to Wanda

your story has b[een]
written for a purpose.
you can trust Him!
Psalm 139:16

Jane Wadl[en]

IT'S A GIFT

Understanding Suffering Through a Biblical Lens

Tami Walker

WESTBOW
PRESS®
A DIVISION OF THOMAS NELSON
& ZONDERVAN

WestBow Press books may be ordered through booksellers or by contacting:

WestBow Press
A Division of Thomas Nelson & Zondervan
1663 Liberty Drive
Bloomington, IN 47403
www.westbowpress.com
844-714-3454

ISBN: 978-1-6642-6515-8 (sc)
ISBN: 978-1-6642-6514-1 (e)

Library of Congress Control Number: 2022907858

Print information available on the last page.

WestBow Press rev. date: 05/13/2022

Suffering is such a hard topic to explore, and it is even harder to live out. Tami has done both with discernment and grace. She has laid out an incredible biblical theology of suffering with the empathy of one who has suffered greatly herself. If you are personally experiencing suffering or are helping another navigate great pain, this is the book for you. Tami's stories and biblical wisdom will give you fresh perspective and comfort.

- Kevin Boer, Network Coach Trainer, National Network of Youth Ministries

"Everyone will face times of difficulty in their life, not many can articulate the beauty of God's unfailing grace in those trials. Tami does exactly that in this book. I am thankful for her honesty and ability to breathe fresh life into the experience of suffering in a way we can all relate to."

- Matt Thrift, Pastor of Student Ministries at South Mountain Community Church in St. George, Utah.

"In this book, *It's a Gift*, Tami Walker excels in comforting and helping her readers understand the difficulties of suffering. She weaves her own tragic and personal struggles together with sound biblical theology and presents them in a kind and caring style. *It's a Gift* is a must read for anyone facing difficult circumstances. Even if you are not in the midst of suffering yourself, this book will provide you with resources for counseling and encouraging those who are."

- G. E. Carlin, D. Min.

"Have you ever asked, 'Why me?' *It's a Gift* is a roadmap that will not only answer this question, but will lead you to accepting that your suffering is actually a gift from our Good Father, as crazy as that sounds. Supported by tons of helpful and hopeful scripture, this book will take you on a bible-based journey through what suffering should look like in the life of a Christian. You won't be disappointed!"

- Tony Wahls, Former Elder at South Mountain Community Church in St. George, Utah

To my mother.
Your victor's crown is within reach.
I love you.

Contents

Acknowledgments xi

Preface xv

Introduction xvii

Chapter 1   The Box: God's Sovereignty In and
             Around Our Suffering 1

Chapter 2   The Promised Gift of Following Jesus 20

Chapter 3   The Gift of Sanctification 29

Chapter 4   The Gift of Discipline 43

Chapter 5   The Gift of Comfort 53

Chapter 6   The Gift of the Gospel 65

Chapter 7   The Gift of Glorifying God 81

Chapter 8   The User Guide: Attitudes In Our Suffering 98

Chapter 9   Wrapped with a Bow: The Promises of God 112

Chapter 10   The Gift of All Gifts 135

Epilogue 143

Reference Notes 151

Acknowledgments

Writing this book was never really a personal dream of mine. It was more of a calling, a calling that my husband saw way before I did. Even then, I ignored it for several years because I felt too inadequate. But they say that God doesn't call the qualified, He qualifies the called. This has been true for me, and I give God all the credit because I know I couldn't have written one single sentence without His guidance. So, first and foremost, my gratitude goes to my Savior, Jesus Christ! But the coolest part in the process of writing this book was the amazing people God placed in my path who played vital parts in making this book a reality. Although I'm going to try, my thanks are going to be inadequate to express the gratitude I have for all of the gifted people who have contributed their time and talents into making this book a reality.

I must first start by thanking my wonderful husband, Phillip. You were the one who first saw the calling and kept encouraging me to follow it, even when I kept telling you "Not a chance!". Writing this book has been as hard as I imagined it would be, yet even more rewarding than I could have imagined with you by my side. None of this would have been possible without you. Thank you for your ever-patient reading and rereading of my drafts, and for all the mornings spent double-checking scripture references with me. Thank you for all your support and encouragement, for your love and devotion. You have sacrificed so much for me and have taken such good care of me. I know I haven't made it easy on you, but you've taken it like a champ! I am eternally grateful.

I've been humbled by the true grammar geniuses on my editing team that have voluntarily and selflessly helped shape this book. I don't know how any author ever properly and thoroughly thanks them, but here are my feeble attempts:

To my son Collin and daughter-in-luv, Kat: There will never be enough ways for me to express my gratitude, or to make you understand how indebted I am to you for the time and energy you both spent editing, then hashing out those edits with me, and allowing yourselves to be my sounding board. Hours and hours were spent. At times, the process was challenging and arduous for all of us, but your encouragement and confidence in me helped keep me going. You both have played some of the most integral parts in the shaping of this book. For that, thank you from the bottom of my heart!

To Genice and Aimee: I am more grateful than you'll ever know for all the time and energy each of you have so willingly invested in me and into this book. I kept asking and you kept giving. I pray that God will richly reward you for all you've done.

To Kevin, Matthew, Tony and Eian: I have treasured your guidance, encouragement, and feedback along the way. Each of you, in your own way and on many levels, have been spiritual mentors in my life, and I am grateful for each of you. They say that true friends tell the truth. Thank you for being my friends.

To the numerous friends and family who have offered their prayers on my behalf throughout the writing of this book: God heard your prayers, and I felt them. To each of you (you know who you are), thank you!

To my daughter, Alayna: A very special thank you for all your graphic design advice, but most of all for being on the sidelines cheering me on. You are a joy to my heart.

To my brother Guy: At one time or another, there may have been a pair of scissors stabbed in the back of one of my doll's heads, some ice thrown at yours, and some scuffles on the floor, but I wouldn't trade one day with you as my brother. Thanks for always being there for me when I've needed you.

To Mom and Dad: Thank you for all the sacrifices you've made, for always being behind me, catching me when I fell, and in turn, pushing me where I needed to be pushed. You both have played a big part in who I am today. I praise God that He chose me to be your daughter.

To my Westbow team: Many thanks to everyone for your patience while helping this newbie through this amazing journey.

Preface

There are two things this book is not. First, it is not a self-help book. While I will be sharing my tactics on how I've learned to manage and cope with my own personal pain and suffering, these tactics are 100% grounded in God's Word and do not come from my own strength. Second, since so many people like to think there isn't a God because of all the suffering in the world, I am not writing this in an attempt to prove that God does exist. Rather, the aim of this book, driving every page forward, is to show — by using scripture — how God's sovereignty commissions our pain in order to bring forth His purpose in our lives. More specifically, to better understand our suffering through a Biblical lens.

Suffering is inevitable. It doesn't matter what your demographic is - age, ethnicity, ancestral background, home life, or the religion you came from. Suffering is a part of this experience we call life. And it exists, as we will be learning, because God has deemed purpose behind it for every believer. Even if you don't consider yourself a follower of Christ, and even though this book isn't a self-help book, I still think you will gain something from reading it. So, even though it is grounded in Biblical truth, I still encourage you to continue reading.

So why is this book titled *IT'S A GIFT*? I'm sure this question may have crossed your mind at least once since picking this book up. Well, I chose this title because it really is the foundation to fully understanding *all* suffering in the believer's life. The bedrock verse for this book is Philippians 1:29. It says, "For it has been granted to you on behalf of Christ not only to believe in Him, but also to suffer for Him." Did you hear that? Just as our ability to believe in Christ has been granted/gifted to us, so our suffering for Him has equally been granted/gifted.

The overarching story of redemption — our regeneration, sanctification, and finally our glorification — may not at first glance seem like something that will help you understand your suffering. However, in my own journey of understanding His will and sovereignty in the face of my progressing physical pain and disabilities, this is what has kept me moving forward. As I've studied God's Word throughout the years, I began to see (as illustrated by the verse above) a steady, connecting theme of God's sovereignty in the salvation of, and sanctification in, the lives of His people. How our salvation *and* our suffering work hand in hand to accomplish the end goal for all of God's people: our expectant joy of one day seeing Christ face to face after being conformed into His image. This is what has helped me acknowledge the goodness of God in my life when I can't comprehend or understand what He's doing. As you read this book, my hope is that you will begin to see this same connection also: the connection between your salvation and your suffering working together to accomplish God's purposes and will in your life.

Introduction

I was blessed to have grown up in a home that loved Jesus. Not only were my mother and father dedicated Christians, but most of their family members were as well. My Oma and Opa on my father's side and my Grandmother and Great-grandmother on my mother's side all left lasting impressions of what godly men and women look like. Some of my favorite memories come from when I was just 4 years old. My Oma would often play the piano and sing from her hymnal. My favorite hymn she would play and sing was *Abide with Me*. Even at such a young age, the words of that hymn comforted me while lying awake in the stillness of the night. They gave me an assurance that God was always with me.

Both my father and mother sacrificed a great deal to give me a Christian education. I attended Christian schools from 3rd grade through my junior year of high school. We would have Bible class before the rest of our studies began each day. I was continually being immersed in the Word of God, memorizing it and learning about His grace, His love, and His character. I can't thank my parents enough for this gift they gave me, as I know my faith would not be where it is today without them.

This faith that was instilled in me from such a young age is what kept me secure in God's loving hand as He guided me through some rough years. Just because I grew up in a Christian home didn't mean I had a perfect family. There were very difficult times and numerous obstacles to navigate throughout my childhood, teen years, and into adulthood.

In 8th grade, I *thought* I had my first real heartbreak. His name? Dylan. Oh, I thought my heart would never heal! However, even though they don't feel like it at the time, high school heartbreaks are the farthest thing from real life trauma. Real heartache knows the pain of abandonment or the devastating collapse of the family home. It knows the pain of being physically or emotionally handled without regard. Real heartache knows the pain of financial stress or ruin. It also knows the pain of God's discipline. Real heartache knows the loss of loved ones. It knows of a life-altering diagnosis for you or a loved one. I've experienced all of these — some on multiple occasions. I'm sure many of you have also. That's why you're reading this book. They make the Dylan's of high school look like your favorite childhood toy being mistreated by your brother.

I was 20 years old when I experienced the first death in my family. It was December 5th, 1995. My Oma, who was more like a mother to me than my grandmother, died of pneumonia and other complications while recovering in the hospital after having somewhat of a normal surgery. I was devastated. However, one day later we received even more crushing news.

My husband and I had recently celebrated our 1st anniversary, and I was two weeks away from being full term with our first child, Tyler Uriah. The day after having to tell my Oma goodbye for the last time, I had a routine OB checkup appointment. Tyler had been breech for about a week so he hadn't been as active as usual. (Our Lamaze instructor had told us this was normal for breech babies.) As the nurse took us back to the room for my exam, I mentioned I hadn't felt him moving as normal. She immediately hooked me up to the portable ultrasound machine to check for Tyler's heartbeat. Static. That's all we heard.

My doctor told me she wanted to take Tyler right away, for my protection, but our church and some of our family were advising against this. They were telling us we needed to just pray and believe that Tyler was alive and that I would deliver a healthy baby. Feeling under pressure, I took their advice over my doctor's.

Needless to say, the following week was the longest week of my life. I felt like I was in a nightmare which was impossible to wake from. I didn't feel the freedom to grieve because of the "faith expectations" that were imposed on me. I went on autopilot. We allowed the influence of the people around us to override our judgement, despite the danger I was putting myself in.

By the following Wednesday, I finally went into labor. We had our bags packed and the car seat waiting to bring home our new family member. Twenty-two hours later I gave birth to Tyler Uriah Walker, but the car seat came home empty.

And, as if losing my Oma and our son in the same week wasn't enough, two months later we found out that my mother-in-law had been having severe abdominal pain that she had been hiding. And two more months after that, they discovered she had ovarian cancer. By that time, it had already spread throughout her whole body. When the surgeons went in to remove the tumors they had no other choice but to sew her back up and say they were sorry. She passed three months later.

My husband and I felt like we had got sucker punched and the wind knocked out of us. It was hard to just breathe after enduring three major deaths in the family, all within 9 months. Our hearts were shattered. As I write this, I am still shaken by the devastation of that year alone.

The following year, however, I gave birth to our second son. Though Collin didn't come easy, we finally had something beautiful in our lives! But the following year, we lost our first daughter, Grace, during my second trimester. Same routine OB checkup appointment. Same lifeless static heard from the ultrasound machine. And this was just hours before we were supposed to be at Phil's grandmother's funeral. Almost a repeat from three years earlier.

At least this time around I allowed my doctor to take care of us the way we should have with Tyler. But, unfortunately, not allowing her to do so the first time caused complications and severe uterine infections with each pregnancy, landing me back in the hospital after every delivery. I even almost lost my own life due to these infections. However, despite all of this, God was gracious to us through it all. He miraculously gave us another beautiful baby girl, Alayna, before my doctor told me I shouldn't have another pregnancy.

God was gentle in His reminders that He was walking alongside us through our heartaches. He began reminding us about His sovereignty, and teaching us about His purpose in our pain. He started to instruct us about what real faith looks like: submitting our will to His. Faith is *not* a hyped-up, prayed-up expectation of only one outcome that must end in a miracle, otherwise resulting in defeat because there was not enough faith mustered up by the expectant. Instead, faith is trusting that God has a good plan for us amidst our pain. Phil and I would never have made it through all of our tragedy so early on in our marriage if it weren't for God's grace and mercy.

I'm going to skip 10 years ahead in my story for the sake of brevity. In February of 2005, one month before my 30th birthday, I slowly became paralyzed from my waist down, all within about a week's time. Through a lot of complications and a misdiagnosis, I was finally diagnosed correctly with Multiple Sclerosis.

This diagnosis came out of left field. I was a healthy, fit, and an active young mother. It was hard to wrap my mind around what was happening. However, I do remember while the paralysis was moving up my legs, there was an unexplainable peace from God ebbing and flowing in the midst of all my questions and concerns. Do you know what surprised me the most? I wasn't really afraid. The peace I was experiencing wasn't what someone in my position would normally have experienced. I knew my Savior, and by this point in my life, I had a strong grasp on what it meant to rest in

God's sovereignty while in the middle of this storm of uncertainty. Even though I didn't like what was happening to me, I knew beyond a shadow of a doubt, that no matter what happened, there would be purpose to it and God would use it for His glory in my life.

After my first initial onset and recovery with MS, I went seven years before having my first relapse. During this period of time I was still able to be the typical do-it-all mom. I was proud to keep our home life running smooth. I volunteered regularly at the kids' school. I was athletic, creative, and a social butterfly. Our family loved outdoor activities. Every weekend Phil wasn't working at the Firehouse we would go find another place to explore in our beautiful Southern Utah "backyard". We all loved skiing! I've had the privilege of serving as a keyboardist on a few different worship teams over the years. My husband and I danced, played in a co-ed city softball league, and went to the gym together regularly. I had passions and hobbies that inspired me. Some of them actually brought in extra income for us. I was a vital part of the workings of our family. All of these things gave me purpose and a sense of self-worth.

However, in my mid 30's things started to change....again. I began to wake up with pain that had no business being in my body at my age. I felt old and achy. Pain not only in my joints, tendons, and muscles, but also in parts of my body that I had never paid attention to before. I felt like my body was betraying me.

I would push through the pain. Pain is weakness leaving the body, right? I always thought I had a great work ethic — until I met my husband. Once we were married, the bar had been raised. So now my biggest fear was coming across as lazy. I felt like I was in this strange limbo between being able-bodied and the slow workings of becoming disabled. The "easy" became hard.

Normal conversations became difficult. It became a chore to process what I was hearing while trying to formulate appropriate responses. I started becoming frustrated as word recollection failed me and I couldn't seem to articulate what I was wanting to convey.

(Trust me, this isn't easy when trying to lecture your children!) My memory began failing me. And if you knew me before all of this, you'd have known I prided myself on my memory. I remembered *everything*. (Just ask my husband.) But I began forgetting names, dates, and conversations. I would forget to pay bills. I would do something then completely forget I had already accomplished it, or I would blame someone else for doing it. I began to have panic attacks, not knowing where I was or if my kids were somewhere safe.

Then all the questions came. How bad would my symptoms get? Would they ever go away? What would my future look like if they didn't? How does this fit in with the MS? Is it going to make it worse? If I feel this bad now, what am I going to feel like in five, ten, fifteen years down the road? And on a broader level — how am I supposed to take care of my family and be that vital contributor to our home that I loved being? Is this going to affect my ability to serve our church, school, and community? I'm I going to lose the ability to continue doing the things I love?

I eventually started to share with my husband what was going on, and he immediately went to work trying to find answers for my symptoms. We soon decided, with the help of my doctors, that these were not all symptoms from the MS, but we weren't seeming to find any other answers either. To make a long story short, Phil spent the better part of ten years researching all the possible illnesses, disorders, and diseases that lined up with my symptoms — which continued to grow and get worse as time went on. We tested for everything and anything that either Phil, or my neurologist, came up with. But with every test that came back negative, I felt like I was losing a battle that I was blindly trying to fight.

I won't bore you with all the details of how we finally got to each of my diagnoses ten years in the making, but as you might imagine, each diagnosis was a moment of profound relief. I finally had a name for every symptom that was mysteriously disabling me. People have asked me (surprisingly even a few doctors), "Why is it so important to have a diagnosis?" Believe me when I say, I don't want to have Multiple Sclerosis, which causes severe nerve pain from previous relapses and lasting sensory disturbances from head to foot; Hypermobile Ehlers-Danlos Syndrome, which causes painful micro tears in my connective tissue (muscles, ligaments, and tendons) that has also lead to instability in my joints causing them to dislocate easily, along with instability in my neck; Degenerative Disc Disease/Osteoarthritis in my neck and middle spine; Gadolinium Deposition Disease, which causes deep bone pain, cognitive impairment and migraines; Trigeminal Neuralgia, which causes intense, electric shock-like pain in the lower face and jaw; all along with a few other comorbidities that come with the above territories. There's too many to list them all. But to actually have names to associate all my symptoms with has given me a sense of validation for all the pain that I've suffered on a daily basis for the last decade. Having answers makes it a lot easier to explain to someone why I can't do the things I used to do, or why I have a disability placard when I can still walk without using a cane or wheelchair for short periods of time. Unless one has been in my shoes, no one can begin to understand what this meant for me.

No one is waiting in great expectation to be disabled, at least no one I've met. No one is sitting around saying, "Hey, you know what would be great? Being in unimaginable amounts of pain every day and missing out on doing all the things I love and used to do; having to give up all the passions and hobbies and creativity that were part of my makeup and made me who I was." No! Of course not. No one wants to give up their career or passions. No one enjoys being dependent on someone else for their daily care and income. No one wants to go from being a valuable contributor of the family to being needy and dependent on them. Losing your independence and your sense of identity is an unimaginable loss.

Pain puts pressure on one's faith and stirs up emotions that are hard to confront and sometimes impossible to push back. Pain can often defeat self-confidence and mental strength, resolve and positive attitudes. Long-term illness and chronic pain can cause isolation and feelings of loneliness which can change a person; changing the mind, emotions, and perspectives. The battle with depression can lead to some very dark places. My own personal tangle with it has been brutal. It has been terrifying and very lonely at times. I fight against my own body and battle with my mind because my heart aches for the life I'm no longer capable of physically living. I'm sure there are many of you reading this right now who can relate.

But here's the thing. If I hadn't learned to cling to Jesus and trust in His word in my youth and early adulthood, I know I wouldn't be here today. Psalm 119:92-93 says, "If your law had not been my delight, I would have perished in my affliction. I will never forget your precepts, for by them you have preserved my life." I can personally identify with David's words.

I look back over all the years and see God's hand intertwined through every inch of my pain and depression. He has woven His love and grace through it all. Even on my darkest days I know He is still walking with me. He is always faithful to remind me of His promises and His goodness through my pain. He taught me when I was young about His sovereignty and that I can trust in it. He opened up His Word to me so I can see His sovereign plan at work in my life — how He uses my suffering for my good and for His glory.

This book represents all the "tools" (God's promises) in my "tool box" (God's Word) that I've collected over the years. I go to it when I need reminders of the truth of His love, grace, mercy, goodness and kindness as I am fighting the despair that, at times, threatens to overtake me. I use these truths and promises I've found in His Word to give me the strength I need each day to be victorious. And trust me, I need to *each* and *every* day!

Hebrews, 4:12 says, "For the word of God is alive and active. Sharper than any double-edged sword, it penetrates even to dividing soul and spirit, joints and marrow; it judges the thoughts and attitudes of the heart." 2 Timothy 3:15-17 says, "...you have known the Holy Scriptures, which are able to make you wise for salvation through faith in Christ Jesus. All Scripture is God-breathed and is useful for teaching, rebuking, correcting and training in righteousness, so that the servant of God may be thoroughly equipped for every good work." And finally, Romans 15:4 says, "For everything that was written in the past was written to teach us, so that through the endurance taught in the Scriptures and the encouragement they provide we might have hope."

You see, our emotions can sometimes be in conflict with each other. At least I know this to be true for myself. Even though I know my thoughts and actions shouldn't be influenced by my emotions, it's very difficult *not* to act based on what I'm feeling in the moment. So, how do we combat the negativity that influences our emotions? With the truth found in God's Word. As stated in the above verses, His Word is useful to judge our thoughts and attitudes. It teaches about our salvation through faith found only in Jesus. It instructs, rebukes and corrects our thinking, and trains us in righteousness so we can be equipped to fight when the enemy comes with his lies. And lastly, but certainly not the least, it gives us the encouragement for the hope we have for a forever future with Jesus.

It's like this: I don't always *feel* like God is with me. However, I *know* from His Word that He has promised He will never leave me (Hebrews 13:5). So I go to my "tool box" and I combat the feelings of loneliness with the promise of His presence.

Of all the people in the Bible, I think I can relate to King David the most (apart from the fact that I've never had to run for my life) because even David had to command his spirit to praise God when He didn't feel like it. He was using this same "tool box" long before I was. In fact, God used him to create some of the tools in my box.

Have you read his story? Have you read the songs he wrote in the book of Psalms? God called David a man after His own heart (1 Samuel 13:14). He was a mighty warrior (1 Samuel 16:18) and the anointed King of Israel (1 Samuel 16). God made a covenant with David promising to establish his kingdom forever (2 Samuel 7:12-13; Psalm 89:3-4). All of this makes David sound like he lived an incredibly victorious life, doesn't it? But if you know anything about his story, you know that it was anything but glamorous. He was running for his life for the better part of 13 years before God gave him the throne. He experienced the loss of a child. He knew what it felt like to be disciplined by God because of his sin. He was betrayed by his son, Absalom, and for a second time, had to run and hide for his life. And yet, through all the stress, pain, heartache, depression, and loneliness, he never stopped serving or worshiping God.

I picture David preaching to himself every morning when he awoke; telling himself to "Praise the LORD, my soul; all my inmost being, praise His holy name. Praise the LORD, my soul, and forget not all His benefits" (Psalm 103:1-2). "Why, my soul, are you downcast? Why so disturbed within me? Put your hope in God, for I will yet praise Him, my Savior and my God" (Psalm 42:11). David was diligent and faithful to read the Word of God — his love for scripture being evident in Psalm 119. Of the 150 Psalms, David authored 73 of them. He was continually reminding himself of the promises God had given him, while pouring himself out before God in anguish and worship. If you've read the book of Psalms, then you've felt the tension between his expression of pain and his prayers of faith. But regardless of his feelings, he continued to preach God's promises to himself. And the book of Psalms is an amazing place to start when you need to preach God's promises to yourself as well.

Just as God told the Israelites to remember how He had saved and delivered them out of the hands of Pharaoh (Deuteronomy 4:9), we need daily reminders of His promises and of what He's done for us. How He's brought us up out of our "Egypt," freeing us from our slave masters of sin and death. He told them to do this because He knows how forgetful the human heart and mind can be.

This is what I've had to learn to do. When I start feeling overwhelmed by the constant pain, and I feel like giving up the fight, I have to command my spirit to praise God through it. I have to use His promises to fight the feelings of hopelessness and depression that can start to set in. I don't always do it right away. The pain often makes me forget how to fight. (If this was easy, it wouldn't be called a fight.) But God is faithful to nudge me and remind me that I have His Word as my tool box.

We must be diligent to engage our enemy. We need to be constantly on the lookout for his attacks. Our enemy can take us from a fighter to a fretter in an instant if we are not aware of his tactics and schemes. Our lack of readiness or unwillingness to engage him is his greatest weapon.

One of Satan's favorite tactics is trying to convince us to quit fighting. This temptation to surrender is an attack against our faith and trust in God's sovereignty. It comes in the cover of night during our pain. It is covert. It is quiet. It often sneaks up on us before we can even see it coming.

Surrendering is like a dark alley. It's giving up and waving the white flag. It is a deep, dark hole that is easy to slip and get sucked into. Trust me. As someone with chronic pain day in and day out, I know all too well. Also, ask the guy who just lost his job and now has no way to provide for his family. Ask the kid who doesn't have any friends, is bullied at school, and who's home life is a disaster. Ask the woman who just lost her life-long husband and best friend for 50+ years. Ask the father who just lost his wife and 4 children in a car accident.

Charles Martin says it like this, "Resignation is an Ephesians 6 spirit without a body. It's a 2 Corinthians 10 argument 'that exalts itself against the knowledge of God.' A strong hold. A speculation. A fortress in our mind."[1]

Your weapon is your sword. Your sword is the Word of God.

Pick it up! Use it! Use it to beat back your resignation, your hopelessness, and loneliness. The best advice I ever received was: When fighting the lies of the enemy, with every one of his lies, counter it with two promises of God. Make bookends to crush the lies of Satan.

So when the enemy says things like, "What's the use of fighting? God doesn't really care about what you're going through. In fact, how can He even love you when He's the one allowing you to go through this pain? You might as well give up." The words out of my mouth need to be something like this:

- "Blessed is the man who makes the LORD his trust, who does not turn to the proud, to those who go astray after a lie" (Psalm 40:4; (ESV).
- "Let their lying lips be silenced, for with pride in contempt they speak arrogantly against the righteous" (Psalm 31:18)
- "Greater is He that is in [me] then he who is in the world" (1 John 4:4).
- I am more than conqueror through Him who loves me (Romans 8:37)
- "Praise be to the LORD my rock, who trains my hands for war, my fingers for battle" (Psalm 144:1).
- "You give me strength to attack my enemies and power to overcome their defenses. This God – how perfect are His deeds! How dependable His words! He is like a shield for all those who seek His protection. The LORD alone is God; God alone is our defense. He is the God who makes me strong, who makes my pathway safe. He makes me sure footed as a deer; He keeps me safe on the mountains. He trains me for battle, so I can use the strongest bow. Oh LORD, you protect me and save me; your care has made me great, and your power has kept me safe" (Psalm 18:29-35; GNBDC).

As I stated in the Preface, our salvation and sanctification work together. The foundation on which we can trust God's promises is in the very grace of God, the price Jesus paid for our sin. When I need to preach to myself, I first remind my soul of His life that was given for mine — the price that was paid for me by His blood. Only then can I remind myself of what that price paid, which is the promise of glory, living with Him in the fullness of eternity. Next, His promise to complete the good work He started in me. And finally, because of these first two, I can remind myself that my suffering is a gift. Preaching a gospel of self-help (resourcing one's own efforts to achieve things without the help of others) will only take me further away from the only true help that will keep me from drowning in self-pity. If Christ is left out of my preaching, I will be going into battle ill equipped. But once I set my focus on Christ, then I can go to His promises and see His sovereign purpose to help me fight my battles. It is because of Christ that I even have the right to use these tools in my box. Here are just a few of my favorites that help me preach Christ to myself.

For it has been granted to you on behalf of Christ not
only to believe in Him, but also to suffer for Him.
(Philippians 1:29 - Our bedrock verse)

Being confident of this, that He who began a good work in
you will carry it on to completion until the day of Christ Jesus.
(Philippians 1:6)

Now it is God who makes both us and you stand
firm in Christ. He anointed us, set His seal of
ownership on us, and put His Spirit in
our hearts as a deposit, guaranteeing what is to come.
(2 Corinthians 1:21-22)

I want to know Christ – yes, to know the power of

His resurrection and participation in His sufferings,
becoming like Him in His death.
(Philippians 3:10)

Therefore, since Christ suffered in His body,
arm yourselves also with the same attitude.
(1 Peter 4:1)

The Gift

I don't know about you, but I love giving gifts (and if we are honest, it's just as fun to receive them). There's just something about that classic gift-in-a-box wrapped with a red bow that is so captivating, right? Unfortunately, most gifts that are given and received nowadays come in gift bags. We often don't take the time to wrap gifts like they did in generations past. But when we are given a gift and the wrapping of the box displays exceptional care and attention to detail, we know that the giver was intentional about the gift they are giving. Anticipation grows knowing that what's inside the box must be something incredible, meant just for you.

As you read this book, I'd like for you to imagine our suffering as a gift. The giver is God, and the recipient is you. What's inside the box is pretty heavy; however, the box God chooses is more than able to hold what's inside of it. The box is covered in pristine white paper and wrapped with a crimson red bow. As you move through these pages, I want you to keep this image of God as He lovingly begins to assemble our gift, placing it in His box, and flawlessly wrapping it in preparation to bestow it upon us.

Before we give a gift, the first thing we do is find the right size box, one that is strong enough to hold the gift we are giving. The gift of our suffering is so heavy that only the box of God's sovereignty can contain it. I mentioned before that God has given purpose to our suffering if we are in Christ, and the only way our pain can have purpose is by God's sovereignty holding it — like a box.

After examining the box of God's sovereignty, we will begin to look at the contents of our gift. I would venture to say that one of the most asked questions among Christians is *"Why?"* Why is this happening to me? Why am I suffering? Why did God allow this? As I've studied the Bible on this topic of suffering over the years, I have found six biblical answers to this question of why we suffer. Each reason why is a little gift in and of itself that makes up the whole. They each play a significant part in this gift that Paul talks about in Philippians 1:29 (our bedrock verse). We will look at each one of these *whys* more closely after examining the box, but here's a quick overview:

1. Suffering because we are promised it when following Jesus
2. Suffering for sanctification
3. Suffering for discipline
4. Suffering for the comfort and encouragement of fellow believers
5. Suffering for the Gospel
6. Suffering for God's glory

After exploring the contents of each gift placed in the box of God's sovereignty, we will look at the included "user guide". This user guide outlines the attitudes we should adhere to in our suffering. And finally, we will watch the beautiful bow of God's promises being wrapped around the box.

———— •••••• ————

I'd like to assure you that I'm writing this book just as much for me as I am for you. I need these reminders of God's promises in this book as much as anyone. Trust and faith are easy words until the pressure's on. Living them is hard. The process of surrendering to God is constant. But the only way we can continue to fully trust Him through our pain is to know Him in an intimate and personal way. We must know His word and what He says about His purpose in our pain. There is only one way to do this. David said in Psalm 9:10, "Those who know your name trust in you, for you, LORD, have never forsaken those who seek you."

Life can be so unpredictable. Joys and sorrows. Beautiful blessings and stressful difficulties. Sunshine one day and storms the next. Trials come unexpectedly. Our dreams and plans can change in an instant. We all know this to be true. So how can we find peace in the middle of such turbulence? Well, I pray that if you have this book in your hands and are reading these pages, you will find this answer. I pray that through your own trials you will begin to know God in a more personal way. Also, as you relate what you will be learning about God's sovereignty in your own suffering, and how He works it all out for your good and His glory, I pray the Holy Spirit will awaken you to a deeper reliance in His infinite wisdom and love so you can learn to trust Him more completely with your life and in your own personal circumstances.

Let's get started, shall we?

The Box: God's Sovereignty In and Around Our Suffering

So surely as the stars are fashioned by His hands, and their orbits fixed by Him, so surely are our trials allotted to us: He has ordained their season and their place, their intensity and the effect they shall have upon us. [1]

~ *Charles Spurgeon*

Before jumping into the six *whys*, or rather the six gifts of our suffering, the first thing we need to do is examine the box that contains them: God's sovereignty. We need to focus our eyes on God Himself and what His sovereignty looks like in the midst of His creation. I'll be honest and let you know I feel very inadequate to write this first chapter (Who am I kidding? More like the whole book!). So I will be using a *whole* lot of help from God's Word, along with some of my favorite Bible teachers.

If we are going to talk about anything pertaining to our walk with Christ, God and His sovereignty should always be the starting point. The *Who* always comes before the *why*. The answers to all of life's questions, whether spiritual or physical, who we are in Christ, and how we are to live in accordance with His grace, can be found in God's Word. We must view every area of our lives through the lens of God's revealed character and attributes. This is important because, even if we don't always understand the *whys* of our suffering, we will never be able to accept, or even appreciate them, unless we first learn *who* God says He is in His Word. I like how Jen Wilkin explains this:

> If our reading of the Bible focuses our eyes on anyone other than God, we have gotten backwards the transformation process. Any study of the Bible that seeks to establish our identity without first proclaiming God's identity will render partial and limited help. We must turn around our habit of asking, 'Who am I?'. We must first ask, 'What does this passage teach me about God?', before we ask it to teach us anything about ourselves. We must acknowledge that the Bible is a book about God. [2]

And John MacArthur, Jr., in his book *The Power of Suffering*, explains God's sovereignty "as the foundational lens through which Christians may see all truths in Scripture more clearly." This is the purpose of this book — to understand suffering through a Biblical lens; and more specifically, through the lens of God's sovereignty. John goes on to say, "Knowing about God's sovereignty in all things does not mean we will have comprehensive understanding, but it gives us a proper hope in the midst of the more difficult and less clear aspects of His working in our lives." [3]

God's Sovereignty

Let's start with what God says about Himself:

> The LORD said to him, *"Who gave* human beings
> their mouths? *Who makes* them deaf or mute?
> *Who gives* them sight or makes them blind?
> *Is it not I, the LORD?"*
> (Exodus 4:11, emphasis mine)

> Yes, and from ancient days I Am He.
> *No one can deliver out of my hand.*
> *When I act, who can reverse it?*
> (Isaiah 43:13, emphasis mine)

> Remember the former things, those of long ago;
> *I am God, and there is no other;* I am God,
> and *there is none like me. I make known the end*
> *from the beginning*, from ancient times,
> what is still to come. I say, *"My purpose will stand,*
> and *I will do all that I please."*
> From the east *I summon* a bird of prey;
> from a far-off land, a *man to fulfill my purpose.*
> *What I have said, that I will bring about;*
> *what I have planned, that I will do.*
> (Isaiah 46:9–11, emphasis mine)

I heard it said once that the power to create grants the power to control. Here's a few more verses that drive this home:

> The LORD brings death and makes alive;
> He brings down to the grave and raises up.
> The LORD sends poverty and wealth;
> He humbles and He exalts.
> (1 Samuel 2:6-7)

LORD, the God of our ancestors, are you
not the God who is in heaven? You rule
over all the kingdoms of the nations.
Power and might are in your hand,
and *no one can withstand you.*
(2 Chronicles 20:6, emphasis mine)

Who appointed Him over the earth?
Who put Him in charge of the whole world?
*If it were His intention and
He withdrew His spirit and breath,*
all humanity would perish together
and mankind would return to the dust.
(Job 34:13-15, emphasis mine)

Our God is in heaven;
He does whatever pleases Him.
(Psalm 115:3, emphasis mine)

The LORD does whatever pleases Him,
in the heavens and on the earth,
and the seas in all their depths.
(Psalm 135:6, emphasis mine)

*There is no wisdom, no insight,
no plan that can succeed against the LORD.*
(Proverbs 21:30, emphasis mine)

Consider what God has done:
Who can straighten what He has made crooked?
(Ecclesiastes 7:13, emphasis mine)

For the LORD Almighty has purposed, and who can thwart Him?
His hand is stretched out, and who can turn it back?
(Isaiah 14:27, emphasis mine)

> To the angel of the church in Philadelphia write:
> These are the words of Him who is holy and true,
> who holds the key of David. *What He opens no
> one can shut, and what He shuts no one can open.*
> (Revelation 3:7, emphasis mine)

Things don't just happen. *All* is within the sovereign will of God. A. W. Pink, an early 20th century English Bible teacher and pastor, said:

> To say that God is sovereign is to declare that God is God. The sovereignty of the God of scripture is absolute, irresistible, infinite. When we say that God is sovereign, we affirm His right to govern the universe, which He has made for His own glory, just as He pleases. We affirm that He is under no rule or law outside His own will and nature; that God is a law unto Himself, and that He is under no obligation to give any account of His matters to anyone. Sovereignty characterizes the whole being of God. He is sovereign in all His attributes. He is sovereign in the exercise of His power. His power is exercised as He wills, when He wills, where He wills. This fact is evident on every page of scripture. [4]

Here are more scripture verses that talk about God's sovereignty over man:

> Many are the plans in a person's heart,
> but *it is the LORD's purpose that prevails.*
> (Proverbs 19:21, emphasis mine)

> In their hearts humans plan their course,
> but *the LORD establishes their steps.*
> (Proverbs 16:9, emphasis mine)

The lot is cast into the lap,
but *its every decision is from the LORD*.
(Proverbs 16:33, emphasis mine)

LORD, I know that *people's lives are not their own;
it is not for them to direct their steps.*
(Jeremiah 10:23, emphasis mine)

What is your life? *You are a mist that appears
for a little while and then vanishes.*
Instead, you ought to say, *"If it is the Lord's will,
we will live and do this or that."*
(James 4;14-15, emphasis mine)

Every plan and decision we make, every trial we encounter, ultimately is traceable back to God our Father. Some people interpret this as Christian fatalism — the lazy attitude that says, "Whatever will be will be, so why bother." However, I'm not here to argue how these scriptures about God's sovereignty over all things do or do not fall under the fatalistic definition, nor how man's free will plays a part. For now, I'm simply pointing out what scripture says.

Submitting to God's Sovereignty

So, in light of all the scripture I've laid out for us so far, how do we handle God's sovereignty? First, we must come to an understanding that no one can fully know or understand God's mind or character. God is infinite in all His ways as well as His being. One of my favorite authors, Jerry Bridges, expresses it this way in his book *Trusting God*: "A finite mind simply cannot comprehend this Infinite Being beyond what He has expressly revealed to us in His Word. Because of this, some things about God will forever remain a mystery to us."[5] Therefore, our ignorance is not an excuse for our lack of trust.

How great is God –
beyond our understanding!
The number of His years is past finding out.
(Job 36:26, emphasis mine)

"For my thoughts are not your thoughts,
neither are your ways my ways",
declares the Lord. "As the heavens are higher
than the earth, so are *my ways higher than your*
ways and my thoughts than your thoughts."
(Isaiah 55:8-9, emphasis mine)

Oh, *the depth* of the riches *of the wisdom*
and knowledge of God!
How unsearchable His judgments,
and *His paths beyond tracing out!*
(Romans 11:33, emphasis mine)

For who knows a person's thoughts except their
own spirit within them? In the same way *no one*
knows the thoughts of God except the Spirit of God.
(1 Corinthians 2:11, emphasis mine)

Secondly, we must adopt the right view of God's justice. There
is no standard higher than God Himself by which to judge. God
Himself is the standard. God is God! You are not.

The LORD said to Job: *"Will the one who*
contends with the Almighty correct Him?
Let him who accuses God answer Him!
… Brace yourself like a man;
I will question you, and you shall answer me.
Would you discredit my justice?
Would you condemn me to justify yourself?"
(Job 40:1-2, 7-8, emphasis mine)

> *But who are you, a human being, to talk back to God?*
> Shall what is formed say to the one
> who formed it, "Why did you make me like this"?
> (Romans 9:20, emphasis mine)

I will be the first to admit that it is difficult to trust God when we are in the middle of a crisis. But trusting God in these times cannot stem from our emotions. It must come from our resolve to believe what God has revealed to us in His Word. Until this happens, we will never truly be able to trust God the way we ought to.

Does it ever feel more difficult to trust God than to obey Him? It definitely has for me at times. During times of distress, when we need to trust God the most, His sovereign will (what we've read about so far) often appears irrational, as opposed to His revealed will. If we are completely honest, even if we don't like it at times, His revealed will (the places in the Bible that tell us how we should live our lives in accordance with His grace) seems reasonable and helps us work out our obedience to Him. But trusting God often has to be worked out in the secret places of God's sovereign will.

> *The secret things belong to the LORD* our God,
> but *the things revealed belong to us*
> and to our children forever,
> that we may follow all the words of this law.
> (Deuteronomy 29:29, emphasis mine)

The Providence of God

The doctrine of God's sovereignty in and over all His creation is called Divine Guidance, or Divine Providence, or again, The Providence of God. These terms have traditionally been understood as: God's supreme rule, guidance, and guardianship over all His creation; the gracious, unceasing outworking of His purpose that governs the universe; a loving Father, in His wisdom, who protects and provides for His children. I like how J. I. Packer, a well-known theologian, defined Providence.

> The unceasing activity of the Creator whereby, in overflowing bounty and goodwill, He upholds His creatures in ordered existence, guides and governs all events, circumstances, and the free acts of angels and men, and directs everything to its appointed goal, for His own glory. [6]

Nothing, not even a tiny little virus, can escape His care and control. (Ironically, I am writing this at the beginning of 2021, 10 months into the COVID pandemic that has devastated lives all around the globe.)

One misplaced understanding of the *Providence of God* is the belief that God is mostly a bystander in our lives and will only step in when necessary. This idea diminishes God's control over our lives which can lead to a belief that when good things are not happening, we just become victims of our fate, or of unfortunate circumstances. This belief can be conscious or unconscious.

Secondly, it can be misused to mean things it is not. For example, it can be used in the context of *only* good things happening to people. Most people would not ascribe providence to anything *bad* happening in their lives. People are usually very uncomfortable, or will even refuse to, assign these events to God's wise and gracious plan for them. However, scripture gives us a very different view of God's governing, not only in the *good*, but also in the *bad* events that play out in our lives. Here are a few of them:

> See now that I myself am He!
> There is no god besides me.
> *I put to death and I bring to life,*
> *I have wounded and I will heal,*

and no one can deliver out of my hand.
(Deuteronomy 32:39, emphasis mine)

When times are good, be happy;
but when times are bad, consider this:
God has made the one as well as the other.
Therefore, no one can discover
anything about their future.
(Ecclesiastes 7:14, emphasis mine)

*Who can speak and have it happen if the LORD
has not decreed it?* Is it not *from the mouth of the
Most High* that *both* calamities and good things *come?*
(Lamentations 3:37–38, emphasis mine)

I formed the light and create darkness,
*I bring prosperity and create disaster,
I, the LORD, do all these things.*
(Isaiah 45:7, emphasis mine)

For some people, these verses can be found offensive. It can bring into question how God can be both loving and good when He Himself claims to be the author of both "calamities and good things". However, the Bible is complete and infallible. It is the very words breathed from God Himself. Therefore, we must allow it to speak for itself, and not insert what we want (or take out what we don't want) it to say.

I know you're probably thinking that I'm sitting in a bubble while writing this book. I thank God that, even though having to experience some very difficult trials of my own, I have not personally been affected by any of the atrocities and horrors that play out in our world. However, I do have a husband who is a firefighter/first responder, I have family members who are in law enforcement, and I have a mother who endured an evil and horrifically abusive childhood. I understand. I hear their stories. The things they have had to endure and the things they have to see every day at their jobs are sickening and disturbing.

I understand the disconnect we in our humanity naturally embrace when it comes to God and the evil we see in the world. I get how hard it is to reconcile the two. Nonetheless, we've just seen from the scripture verses above that whatever God does is good. This should be an uncontested statement for those who claim to be in Christ. God does many things that don't line up with our perceptions. But when we take into question His claim of authorship in both good and calamity it only reveals a deficiency in our own comprehension of His goodness in and through such things.

Here's the thing. How is it possible to trust God if His power is limited? Or, just the opposite. How can we trust Him if He chose not to use His unlimited power to guide us? Again, Jerry Bridges helps qualify this:

> If there is a single event in all of the universe that can occur outside of God's sovereign control, then we cannot trust Him. His love may be infinite, but if His power is limited and His purpose can be thwarted, we cannot trust Him. [7]

God, in His infinite and perfect wisdom, is working out His plan in our lives. It is almost always going to be beyond our ability to comprehend. Therefore, we must learn to trust Him, *especially* when we do not understand. As His children, our only option is to submit to His authority and rest in His care. We may not have the answers or understand why God allows evil, but we can rest assured that He is all powerful and knows how to work out everything He gives us for our good and for His glory.

So rather than being offended by this, we should instead actually seek to find comfort in it. We may be assured that God has a loving purpose in both our blessings *and* our adversity. As King Hezekiah said, "Surely it was for my benefit that I suffered such anguish" (Isaiah 38:17). King Hezekiah is recognizing that his suffering and anguish came from the hand of God and was for his own benefit. If he can recognize it (along with Joseph, King David, Peter, Paul, and even Jesus himself) we should strive to do the same, no matter how uncomfortable it may be or how much it assaults our idea of how we think a loving God should act.

God's Goodness in Our Suffering

Let's start by looking at some more scriptures that talk about God's goodness in our suffering:

> You intended to harm me,
> but *God intended it for good*
> *to accomplish what is now being done.*
> (Genesis 50:20, emphasis mine)

> Naked I came from my mother's womb,
> and naked I will depart.
> *The LORD gave and the LORD has taken away;*
> may the name of the LORD be praised.
> (Job 1:21, emphasis mine)

> I know, LORD, that your laws are righteous,
> And that *in faithfulness you have afflicted me.*
> (Psalm 119:75, emphasis mine)

> *All the days ordained for me*
> [good and bad] were written in Your book
> *before one of them came to be.*
> (Psalms 139:16, emphasis mine)

Therefore, in order to keep me from becoming
conceited, *I was given* a thorn in my flesh...to torment me.
(2 Corinthians 12:7, emphasis mine)

So then, *those who suffer according to God's will*
should commit themselves to their *faithful
Creator* and continue to do good.
(1 Peter 4:19, emphasis mine)

Though *He brings grief,* He will show compassion,
so great is His unfailing love. For *He does not
willingly bring affliction or grief* to anyone.
(Lamentations 3:32–33, emphasis mine)

I believe the verse above in Lamentations needs to be unpacked before we move on because it can seem like there is a contradiction. Jeremiah is first stating that God Himself *brings grief,* but in the very next sentence he is saying that God *does not willingly bring grief.* Maybe I can help illustrate this by using a parent/child relationship.

A kind, loving, and gentle parent in their wisdom, will discipline their child in order to build and refine their character. If you were fortunate enough to have a mother and/or father who cared enough about your character, or, if you have your own children and care enough about theirs, you should be able to understand this.

No discipline is pleasant at the time, and loving discipline will still bring pain and grief to the child. However, this discipline does not come from a place of evil intent to harm the child. When I disciplined my children, my purpose wasn't to harm them out of spite. My purpose was to help them grow and learn from their mistakes by assigning appropriate consequences for their actions. Only an abusive parent would purposefully, and willingly, bring harsh punishment on his children with no good intentions associated with it.

So here, Jeremiah is backing up his first statement about God being the one who brings grief with a second statement to make sure we understand that it does not come from a place of ill will. God, our Father, is willing to discipline us, His children, for good intent. He is never willing to discipline us out of harmful intent.

One of the most quoted verses in the book of Romans speaks to this very topic: "And we know that *in all things God works for the good of those who love Him*, who have been called according to His purpose" (Romans 8:28, emphasis mine). This verse will never get old. This is a promise to us, His people; not to those who reject Him, but for those who *love Him*. This understanding should bring so much comfort to us in our times of trial and pain. This is a promise of His love, His wisdom, and His sovereignty over our lives...*even* in our suffering.

God only has our best interests in mind. We can trust Him that He has prepared good things for us. We just need to be careful not to insert our own ideas of what *good* looks like for ourselves.

Since ancient times no one has heard,
no ear has perceived, no eye has seen any *God* besides you,
who *acts on behalf of those who wait for Him*.
(Isaiah 64:4, emphasis mine)

Here is Paul quoting Isaiah:

However, as it is written: "What no eye has seen,
what no ear has heard, and what *no human mind has
conceived*— *the things God has prepared
for those who love Him*."
(1 Corinthians 2:9, emphasis mine)

The Fear of God and Humility of Heart

The fundamental principle that should guide us in all this is:
any view of God, which does not lead us to the fear of God,
cannot be a biblical view of God. [8]
~ Robert A Morey

We do not serve God because of what He does for us, but because of *who He is*. It would be like my children loving me only because of the good things I provide for them, not for who I am as their mother. We must have an awe and reverent love and fear of God, the Sovereign Creator of the universe that breathed life into our lowly, finite bodies. This should be humbling. And this should be the first and foremost motivation of our hearts: to love and worship Him whether or not we like how He's working in our lives. I like what James R. White says about loving and worshiping God in truth:

> Do we love God—all of God, including the "tough" parts of His nature—or do we refuse to bow before those elements that cause us "problems"? If we love Him and worship Him as He deserves, we will not dare to "edit" Him to fit our desires. Instead, we will seek to worship Him in truth. [9]

When we cultivate this holy fear, loving and worshiping Him as He reveals Himself in scripture, it will help us put our suffering into perspective. In his book, Fearing God, Dr. Robert Morey says:

> What is wisdom? The ability to see something from God's viewpoint. And what is understanding? The ability to respond to what you have seen according to God's word. [10]

The command to fear God, or the phrase *God-fearing,* appears roughly 300 times in the Bible. In the book of Proverbs, the fear of the Lord is referred to 15 times as being the source of wisdom, knowledge, discretion, truthfulness, and morality. Here are a few of my favorite verses that describe the benefits to fearing God:

And He [God] said to the human race,
"The fear of the Lord — that is wisdom,
and to shun evil is understanding."
(Job 28:28, emphasis mine)

*The angel of the LORD encamps around
those who fear Him*, and He delivers them.
Taste and see that the LORD is good;
blessed is the one who takes refuge in Him.
Fear the Lord, you His holy people,
for *those who fear Him lack nothing*.
(Psalm 34:7-9, emphasis mine)

For as high as the heavens are above the earth,
so great is His love for those who fear Him;
as far as the east is from the west, so far has He
removed our transgressions from us. As a father
has compassion on his children, so t*he LORD
has compassion on those who fear Him*...
But from everlasting to everlasting *the Lord's
love is with those who fear Him*.
(Psalm 103:11-13, 17, emphasis mine)

The fear of the LORD is the beginning of knowledge,
but fools despise wisdom and instruction.
(Proverbs 1:7, emphasis mine)

The fear of the Lord is the fountain of life,

turning a man from the snares of death.
(Proverbs 14:27, emphasis mine)

He will be the sure foundation for your times,
a rich store of salvation and wisdom and knowledge;
the fear of the LORD is the key to this treasure.
(Isaiah 33:6, emphasis mine)

Possessing the fear of God is an absolute necessity for living in humility and submission. We need to believe everything God has revealed to us in His word. Only pride sets itself up against God and refuses to accept His sovereignty over *all* things. We would do well to learn this lesson from Job:

> Then Job replied to the Lord: *"I know that you can do all things*; no purpose of yours can be thwarted. You asked, 'Who is this that obscures My plans without knowledge?' Surely *I spoke of things I did not understand, things too wonderful for me to know.* You said, 'Listen now, and I will speak; I will question you, and you shall answer me.' My ears had heard of you *but now my eyes have seen you. Therefore I* despise myself and *repent* in dust and ashes." (Job 42:1-6, emphasis mine)

Here's another lesson on humility that we can learn. This is from the gentile king of Babylon, whom God used to punish His people (Jeremiah 27:5-7). Several years after King Nebuchadnezzar captured Jerusalem (Daniel 1:2), God put him in his rightful place. This is what King Nebuchadnezzar had to say afterward:

> At the end of that time, I, Nebuchadnezzar, raised my eyes towards heaven, and my sanity was restored. Then I praised the Most High; I honored

and glorified Him who lives forever. His dominion is an eternal dominion; His kingdom endures from generation to generation. All the peoples of the earth are regarded as nothing. He does as He pleases with the powers of heaven and the peoples of the earth. No one can hold back His hand or say to Him: "What have you done?" At the same time that my sanity was restored, my honor and splendor were returned to me for the glory of my kingdom. My advisers and nobles sought me out, and I was restored to my throne and became even greater than before. Now I, Nebuchadnezzar, praise and exalt and glorify the King of Heaven, because everything He does is right and all His ways are just. *And those who walk in pride He is able to humble.* (Daniel 4:34–37, emphasis mine)

We are sinning when we shake our fists at God and angrily make accusations at Him. Nevertheless, to clarify, I believe there is nothing wrong with asking God *why*. We just need to watch our approach. We must remember to *Whom* we are asking.

Conclusion

I heard someone once say that if we have been given a gift, we should probably do our best to get to know the one who gave it. Our gift of suffering hangs upon the very character of God. If we don't put in the effort to get to know Him the way He has revealed Himself to us in His Word, we will never be able to find the peace that comes with the understanding that God has given purpose to our suffering.

Even though God's purposes are not simple, we can be comforted by the very fact that we will never find ourselves somewhere that the sovereignty of God has not already purposed and directed for His own glory and for our eternal benefit. This should be a major distinguishing factor between the suffering of believers from unbelievers: our suffering has meaning and purpose in God's eternal plan.

More times than not, we won't have answers to the whys of our suffering, but trusting God often means living without the answers to them. And, again, it is during these seasons, when we do not understand, that we must be careful not to replace the Word of God with our fallible interpretations of it. If we could fully know and understand all of who God is and all of His reasonings then God would not be God. His sovereignty and His paths of Providence will always be a mystery, but "[His] word is a lamp for [our] feet, [and] a light on [our] path" (Psalm 119:105). The only source of our comfort in living without our *whys*, is knowing that we can trust *Who*.

⸻ ⋅◆◆◆⋅ ⸻

I keep asking that the God of our Lord Jesus Christ, the glorious Father,
may give you the Spirit of wisdom and revelation,
so that you may know Him better.

EPHESIANS 1:17

The Promised Gift of Following Jesus

In this world you will have trouble.
But take heart! I have overcome the world.

JOHN 16:33

The six *whys* of our suffering (these small gifts that make up the whole) aren't necessarily in any particular order. However, if there was a specific order, I believe this one would need to be first.

So many Christians think we should not experience hardships when we start walking with Jesus. They think life should get easier, not harder. They think that a victorious life in Christ should look, well, victorious. Victors don't ever look defeated, right? And some of these people will even tell you that if you do look defeated then something is wrong with you; or at least, something is wrong with your faith. And then others will often surmise that God allows suffering in the believers life but He doesn't plan it. Well, to both of these, we will actually see (again) the opposite in scripture as we go through this chapter.

In my opinion, one of the first things a new Christian should be taught is that the road marked out for them is not going to be easy. The Christian is promised suffering in this life. They cannot assume to completely escape it yet still share in the benefits of Christ's suffering. We see in our opening quote that Jesus wasn't being ambiguous when He told His disciples that they would have trouble in this world. No, He was straightforward. He never hid the cost. There was no fine print. Being His disciple was a promise of suffering. Discipleship will always demand sacrifice.

The Promise of Suffering for the Believer

Yes, there will be good times, gracious provision, victories over sin, and blessings that come from our Father. However, we are promised, even more so *called*, to a life of suffering. We see that Paul is pretty straightforward in this message to the Thessalonica church. He tells them:

> We sent Timothy…to strengthen and encourage
> you in your faith, so that no one would
> be unsettled by these trials.
> *For you know quite well that we are destined for them.*
> (1 Thessalonians 3:2-3, emphasis mine)

In this next verse, David affirms what he knew about the days that were ordained for him, before he was even conceived within his mother's womb — every good day, every bad day, every victory, and every battle that would reside within them. He tells God:

> Your eyes saw my unformed body; *all the*
> *days ordained for me were written*
> *in your book before one of them came to be.*
> (Psalm 139:16, emphasis mine)

We too are the main characters of our own individual book that God has written. Every single day of our lives, good and bad, from conception to death, has been written and ordained by the Author before we were ever born.

As the title of this book infers, suffering has been given to us. It was determined from the beginning that suffering would be granted to Christ's followers, alongside the faith to believe in Him. Just in case you need another reminder, here's our bedrock verse again.

> *For it has been granted* to you on behalf of Christ
> not only to believe in him but *also to suffer for Him.*
> (Philippians 1:29, emphasis mine)

Pick Up Your Cross and Follow Me

*Then He called the crowd to Him along with His disciples and said:
"Whoever wants to be my disciple must deny themselves
and take up their cross and follow me."*

MARK 8:34

Often people use the phrase, "This is my cross to carry," meaning they have a burden to bear, such as a strained relationship or a thankless and mundane job. Although these can be difficult and used by God to build our character, this is not what Jesus meant when He told His disciples to take up their cross and follow Him. In fact, in the 11th chapter of Matthew He actually tells us *not* to carry those kinds of burdens (Matthew 11:28-30). When He told His disciples (and to anyone within hearing distance) to pick up their cross and follow Him, He was actually calling them to "die to self" (die to their fleshly desires) on a daily basis. It was a call to surrender. Listen to the language Jesus used after the call (which, ironically, was just after telling His disciples that He Himself would soon suffer and die).

Then He said to them all: "Whoever wants to be my disciple must deny themselves and take up their cross daily and follow me. *For whoever wants to save their life will lose it, but whoever loses their life for me will save it.* What good is it for someone to gain the whole world, and yet lose or forfeit their very self? *Whoever is ashamed of me* and my words, *the Son of Man will be ashamed of them* when He comes in His glory and in the glory of the Father and of the holy angels." (Luke 9:23-26, emphasis mine)

Now, after reading the context, can you see what it really means to pick up your cross and follow Him? If you really want *the* good life here on earth, you will lose your life in the end when it matters the most. But, if you *really* want to save your life, then you will lose it now — walk away from it, if necessary — for the sake of Christ. Essentially, Jesus is saying to us, "If you want to follow me, you must understand that you may face losing friends, family, reputation, your job, and possibly even your life. So, which will it be? Me, or you and your comforts?" For some, the cost is too high. They love their lives too much to give them up and follow Jesus (see Luke 9:57-62 and John 6:60-69). In an article called *The School of Suffering*, Josef Tson wrote:

> Personally, I have a problem with certain preachers who say, "Come to Jesus and all your problems will be solved." I do not find that message in the New Testament. I find a Christ who says, "Before following Me, stop and ponder. You have to enter a narrow gate, to walk a narrow path with very few on it. You will be hated because of Me. I am poor, poorer than a fox. You must know whom you follow. And you must know that it involves taking a cross daily. A cross means dying. Make your mind up and only then follow. [1]

I heard it said once that Christ not only died to make us alive, He made us alive so that we too may die. Then, once we have died in Christ, only then will we truly live. Read this again.

"He Himself bore our sins" in His body on the cross,
so that we might die to sins and live for righteousness.
(1 Peter 2:24, emphasis mine)

Now if we are children, then we are heirs
— heirs of God and co-heirs with Christ,
if indeed we *share in His sufferings in order that we
may also share in His glory.* I consider that
*our present sufferings are not worth
comparing with the glory* that will be revealed in us.
(Romans 8:17-18, emphasis mine)

*We always carry around in our body the death of Jesus so
that the life of Jesus may also be revealed in our body.*
For we who are alive are always being given over
to death for Jesus' sake, *so that His life may
also be revealed in our mortal body.*
(2 Corinthians 4:10-11, emphasis mine)

*I have been crucified with Christ and I no longer live,
but Christ lives in me.* The life I now live in the body, I live by
faith in the Son of God who loved me and gave Himself for me.
(Galatians 2:20, emphasis mine)

I want to know Christ – yes, to know
the power of His resurrection *and
participation in His sufferings becoming
like Him in His death*, and so, somehow,
attaining to the resurrection from the dead.
(Philippians 3:10-11, emphasis mine)

> *For you died*, and your life is now hidden *with Christ*
> in God. When Christ, who is your life, appears,
> then *you also will appear with Him in glory*.
> (Colossians 3:3–4, emphasis mine)

> Here is a trustworthy saying: *If we died*
> *with Him, we will also live with Him*.
> (2 Timothy 2:11, emphasis mine)

Following the Suffering Messiah

Even though the path of suffering has been destined, ordained, and granted for us as God's children, we have the comfort in knowing that we are not alone in our trials. Our Master walks with us because He has journeyed the road before us. He knows the way because He was the one that paved the way. In Jesus' High Priestly Prayer, He again expresses not only the requirement that He must suffer, but also His willingness to do so.

> *For them I sanctify myself,*
> *that they too may be truly sanctified.*
> (John 17:19, emphasis mine)

Hebrews 5:8-9 says, "Son though He was, *He learned obedience from what He suffered* and, *once made perfect*, He became the source of eternal salvation for all who obey Him" (emphasis mine). These are two very interesting concepts: Jesus *learning obedience* and being *made perfect*. Here is my understanding of it.

Paul tells us that Jesus limited Himself to experience life on this earth as a human (Philippians 2:6-9). Being human ourselves, we know firsthand the course of life. When we are born we immediately begin maturing physically and intellectually. As we continue to grow, we encounter both pleasant and unpleasant experiences, both blessings and trials. Most of us experience suffering, some more than others. Lastly, we all eventually have to face death. Well, God made sure that His Son was not exempt to these same experiences. He chose the low position of having to physically mature and be taught by other human beings. Thus, Jesus *learned obedience*, not because He was susceptible to disobedience, but so He would fully experience life as we do. As a child, He obeyed His parents (Luke 2:51). As an adult, He obeyed the law and His Father's will (Matthew 5:17; Luke 22:42).

And just like we have to endure suffering in this life, Jesus also chose to undergo suffering. We learn from Scripture that suffering transforms the believer, working to perfect them (Romans 5:3; 2 Corinthians 1:6; James 1:2-3). The writer of Hebrews indicates that after Jesus endured His suffering, He too was *made perfect* by it. However, there is a big difference between our 'being made perfect by way of suffering' and Jesus' 'being made perfect by way of suffering'. Perfect doesn't always mean to be without imperfection. The phrase *made perfect* in Hebrews 5:9, comes from the Greek word *teleios*, which means: to bring to an end, to complete. [2] For Jesus, His 'being made perfect' was completing the purpose for which He came: to live a completely sinless life while undergoing all human frailty and suffering, perfectly finishing His course on humanity. And in doing so "He became the source of eternal salvation for all who obey Him".

If Jesus, being the Son of God, needed to learn obedience from His suffering — needing to be made perfect through it, and be sanctified to obtain His glory — why would sinful man ever wonder why we are called to pass through suffering also? Jesus' suffering teaches us a very important lesson: suffering is necessary, and a true believer will not escape it. If a diamond must be cut to reveal its brilliance, how much more are we to be made perfect without first being split in preparation for the cutting process? God has ordained tribulation to be engraved upon His people. Because Jesus suffered, we too will suffer.

In Peter's first book to the Christians in exile, he tells them, "To this [suffering] you were called, because Christ suffered for you, leaving you an example, that you should follow in His steps" (1 Peter

2:21). He went before us. He lived as an example of how to endure our own path of suffering as He did. He is now our High Priest who is able to sympathize with us in our weaknesses (Hebrews 4:15). If we are going to be victorious through our trials, we must grasp this truth through every agonizing experience — Jesus is with us and is strengthening us, as we follow in His footsteps. We can find joy in our suffering, as He did, because we have hope that there is a reward which is far greater for those who share in His sufferings.

For just as *we share abundantly in the sufferings of Christ*,
so *also our comfort abounds through Christ*.
(2 Corinthians 1:5, emphasis mine)

Let us then approach God's throne of grace
with confidence, so that we may receive mercy
and find grace to help us in our time of need.
(Hebrews 4:16, emphasis mine)

Let us run with perseverance the race marked out for us,
fixing our eyes on Jesus, the pioneer and perfecter of faith.
For the joy set before Him He endured the cross, scorning its
shame, and sat down at the right hand of the throne of God.
Consider Him who endured such opposition from sinners,
so that you will not grow weary and lose heart.
(Hebrews 12:1-3, emphasis mine)

Therefore, since Christ suffered in His body,
arm yourselves also with the same attitude.
(1 Peter 4:1, emphasis mine)

But *rejoice* inasmuch as you participate
in the sufferings of Christ, so that you may *be
overjoyed when His glory is revealed*.
(1 Peter 4:13, emphasis mine)

One of the early martyrs said, "I can bear it all, for Jesus suffered, and He suffers in me now; He sympathizes with me, and this makes me strong." [3] I want to know this suffering Jesus as I suffer.

Conclusion

God's people will have their trials. It was never in God's plan that we should be untested. He tells us through the prophet Isaiah, that we were chosen in the furnace of affliction (Isaiah 48:10). We are not chosen for worldly joys and earthly comforts. Freedom from difficulties, trauma, scars, and bruises was never promised to us. However, there are two things we are promised and can be assured of: our suffering and His presence in them.

The call to every man is to pick up their cross and follow Jesus. This is not a passive statement that Jesus was telling His followers. It requires action. In the Bible, the ones who did follow Him literally dropped everything they were doing to follow Him. They saw the gift. For those of us today, it may not seem to be as literal as it was for His disciples. Regardless, action is still required on our part. If you are *in Christ*, it means you have been called to follow Him. To be *called by Christ* is a summons to lose your life — dying *to self* — to find new life in Him. It's our gift. Although the call is tough, our reward is matchless.

— ·◆◆◆◆· —

May the Lord direct your hearts into God's
love and Christ's perseverance.

2 THESSALONIANS 3:5

The Gift of Sanctification

These trials are for the testing and strengthening of your faith — they are waves that wash you further upon the Rock. [1]

~ Charles Spurgeon

D o you remember reading how Jesus was made perfect through His suffering in the last chapter? Do you remember how it is in a completely different sense that we are made perfect through our suffering? This *suffering for perfection* is called sanctification. Jesus, Himself, refers to suffering (both His and ours) as sanctification in John 17:19. For us, this process of being made perfect through our suffering is not only important, but it is necessary. And it is this necessity that brings us to our second *why, The Gift of our Sanctification.*

I'm going to keep reminding you of our bedrock verse. "For *it has been granted* to you on behalf of Christ not only *to believe in Him*, but *also to suffer for Him*" (Philippians 1:29, emphasis mine). First, God gives us the ability to believe that Jesus died for our sins and the ability to accept Him as our Savior. Second, He gives us the gift of being conformed into His likeness.

Sanctification is the second process in the story of our redemption. The first step is our justification/regeneration, which begins at the very moment of our salvation, the moment of being justified before God through Christ. The very next moment, after your salvation has been applied by the Holy Spirit who now lives in you, sanctification immediately begins the process of taking us from our sinful state to transforming us into the image of Christ. Our salvation is secure in Christ, but as my pastor likes to say, in a sense, it's yet to be complete. There is a lot of refinement that we must go through, a lot of dross that needs to be chiseled off. He doesn't require us to get cleaned up before we come to Him. That is His job! He saves, then He sanctifies.

I like the way Gregg Allison describes the three aspects of the process of redemption in a believer's life:

1. Positional - An immediate setting apart from sin and for God's purpose upon salvation.
2. Progressive - Ongoing process of becoming more like Jesus that will continue until death.
3. Perfected – Upon death, Christians become like Christ, completed in salvation, including their glorified bodies. [2]

Here's one of my favorite verses that speaks to this process:

> Being confident of this, that He who *began*
> *a good work* in you *will carry it on to*
> *completion* until *the day of Christ Jesus.*
> (Philippians 1:6, emphasis mine)

First, He *begins the good work.* This is His regeneration of our hearts (Ezekiel 11:19; 36:25-27), and the making us into a new creation (2 Corinthians 5:17).

Second, He promises to *accomplish/complete this work* He started. He does this by using the method of sanctification, which is His

Spirit living and working inside of us to fashion us into His image (Hebrews 2:11).

Third, He does it all for *the day of Christ Jesus* — the commencement of the believer's glorification with Him (Acts 20:32; Colossians 1:12).

> God chose you as firstfruits *to be saved*
> *through the sanctifying work of the Spirit*
> *and through belief* in the truth.
> (2 Thessalonians 2:13, emphasis mine)

> *For it is God who works in you* to will and
> to act in order *to fulfill His good purpose*.
> (Philippians 2:13, emphasis mine)

> For by one sacrifice He has made perfect
> forever *those who are being made holy*.
> (Hebrews 10:14, emphasis mine)

These three verses quoted above use very progressive language. The phrases "through the *sanctifying work*," "God *who works*," and "who are *being made* holy," indicate an action or condition that is continuing in the present. Mary Wiley uses this same language when speaking about sanctification:

> The majority of scripture about sanctification focuses on progressive sanctification, which starts at the beginning of our new life in Christ and ends with our physical life on earth. It's walking with Christ and seeking to live a life that honors him. This is not a linear process but an upward process. [3]

For the Testing of Faith, Growth, and Fruit

Our Lord in His infinite wisdom and superabundant love,
sets so high a value upon His people's faith that He will not
screen them from those trials by which faith is strengthened...
You are a tree that never would have rooted so well if the wind
had not rocked you to and fro, and made you take firm hold
upon the precious truths of the covenant grace. [4]

~ Charles Spurgeon

One of my favorite things to see is a well thought out and planned landscape or garden. Gardening fascinates me. Maybe it's because I'm amazed there are people out there that have a gift I did not receive – keeping things alive. However, even though I don't know much beyond seed-in-good-soil-with-sun-and-water-grows, it amazes me when I see a newly landscaped area where the tree saplings are planted without stakes. I may not know much, but I do know that new trees need support as they begin to root. The tree in Spurgeon's quote above is a perfect metaphor relating our growth through suffering to a tree's growth through storms.

I think it's safe to say that we've all seen newly planted trees tied to stakes for support, but have you ever looked close enough to see that the tree is only loosely tied to its stakes? Though the stakes are there for support, room must be left for this new sapling to grow on its own amidst life's storms. The gardener leaves room for the tree to be shaken, so that someday it will become unshakable. It is only when he feels that the sapling has grown into a healthy, strong, and rooted tree, and has developed enough resistance to stand on its own, that he will he remove the stakes. Once this happens, the tree is now well enough established to withstand the heavy winds of the coming storms.

> But whose delight is in the law of the Lord,
> and who meditates on His law day and night.
> *That person is like a tree* planted *by streams of water,*
> *which yields its fruit in season* and *whose leaf*
> *does not wither* – whatever they do prospers.
> (Psalm 1:2-3, emphasis mine)

The author of Psalm 1 speaks of a person (likened to a tree which is *planted by streams of water)* who establishes himself firmly in the Word of God. In doing so, the author implies that even though this person will go through seasons of yielding fruit, he will not wither because he delights in and meditates on God's Word. Another benefit from this person being firmly planted is that the fruit which he yields is promised to be prosperous. Paul tells us what this yielded fruit looks like in Galatians 5:22-23: "But the fruit of the Spirit is love, joy, peace, forbearance (which is patience/long-suffering), kindness, goodness, faithfulness, gentleness and self-control."

Jesus uses this gardening metaphor about vines. He says:

> "I am the true vine, and my Father is the gardener.
> He cuts off every branch in me that bears no fruit,
> while *every branch that does bear fruit He prunes so*
> *that it will be even more fruitful*... I am the vine; you
> are the branches. If you *remain in me and I in you,*
> *you will bear much fruit*; apart from me you can do
> nothing." (John 15:1-2 & 5, emphasis mine)

In nature, if a tree or vine doesn't get pruned, it will not produce good fruit. Pruning is the process of removing all the deadwood, damaged branches, and diseased leaves from a fruit-bearing tree or plant. By doing so, you prioritize the healthier parts. When the deadwood is cut off, it stimulates the growth of new fruiting wood. This fruiting wood then creates more fruit spurs (the short twigs) that will eventually bear the fruit. So it is with us.

In 1 Corinthians, Paul uses the training that athletes undergo as a metaphor to our own life of sanctification. He tells us to run the course before us to obtain the prize.

> Do you not know that in a race all the runners run, but only one gets the prize? *Run in such a way as to get the prize.* Everyone who competes in the games goes into strict training. They do it to get a crown that will not last, but we do it to get a crown that will last forever. Therefore I do not run like someone running aimlessly; I do not fight like a boxer beating the air. No, I strike a blow to my body and make it my slave so ... I myself will not be disqualified for the prize (1 Corinthians 9:24-27, emphasis mine).

As an athlete myself in high school and as a young adult, I would train and push myself to the limit. I knew that when I stretched myself I got stronger and more proficient in my skills. There was a goal to achieve, and I knew a champion is not made on a comfortable couch. And the JV girls volleyball team I coached didn't make it to the end of their season undefeated because I let them play Hopscotch and Kick the Can. I made them work hard for their title, on *and* off the court. But the best part was that they wanted it. They knew what it was going to take, and so they chose for themselves to "run in such a way as to get the prize."

I think of my son and his wife as another good example. They are avid rock climbers and enjoy many of the rock climbing crags here in Southern Utah. Every time they go climbing they have an objective: to send a higher grade (climb without falling) than the one they climbed before. There are other ways they could reach the top that could save them a lot of time and energy, but what drives them is the conquest, not ease of achieving their goal. They want to reach their intended objective of climbing to the top by doing it the hard way, which in doing so tests their strength, character, and resolve.

Both Jesus and Paul use the metaphor of birth pains (John 16:21; Romans 8:19-25). Labor pains stretch a woman's body to get her ready for birth. I love all of these metaphors because we can witness the process of growth through pain and see their fruit as a result. Every prize that's worth celebrating requires pain.

A true born-again believer in Christ must know this: trials, sorrows, and difficulties cause humility, submission, and dependence. It is difficult, and this is good. It's not easy, but we are growing. This is the process that transforms and refines us into His image.

Consider it pure joy, my brothers and sisters,
whenever you face *trials of many kinds*, because you know
that *the testing of your faith produces perseverance.*
Let perseverance finish its work so that you may be
mature and complete, not lacking anything.
(James 1:2-4, ESV, emphasis mine)

And we boast in the hope of the glory of God.
Not only so, but we also glory in our sufferings,
because we know that *suffering produces perseverance;
perseverance, character; and character, hope.*
And hope does not put us to shame, because God's
love has been poured out into our hearts through
the Holy Spirit, who has been given to us.
(Romans 5:2-5, emphasis mine)

We are distressed...which *produces in you
patient endurance* of the same sufferings we suffer.
(2 Corinthians 1:6, emphasis mine)

In these verses above, both James and Paul are saying when true faith is tested it should generate perseverance, or patient endurance.

As we persevere through our trials, knowing we are under God's gracious hand, our *muscles* are being stretched, which in turn begins to build our character. The more our perseverance and character are built, the more capacity we have to endure; the more we rely, trust, and hope in our Savior.

While the wheat sleeps comfortably in the husk it is useless to man, it must be threshed out of its resting place before its value can be known. Thus it is well that the Lord tests the righteous, for it causeth them to grow rich toward God." [5]

~ *Charles Spurgeon*

Self-Reliance vs. God-Reliance

Often, when it comes to our own shaking, our own pressure and pain, it seems strange, unconventional, and sometimes unfair. It can also often produce pride. Here's an example. I absolutely cringe when I hear the "Christianese" phrase, "God won't give you any more than you can handle." It's completely unbiblical and sets up the one who is suffering to fall into self-reliance. They are essentially being told, "You don't need God. You can handle this on your own. God wouldn't have allow it to happen otherwise." Well, let's see what Paul has to say about this:

> We do not want you to be uninformed, brothers and sisters, about the troubles we experienced in the province of Asia. We were under great pressure, *far beyond our ability to endure*, so that we despaired of life itself. Indeed, *we felt we had received the sentence of death. But this happened that we might not rely on ourselves but on God*, who raises the dead. He has delivered us from such a deadly peril, and He will deliver us again. *On Him we have set our hope that He will continue to deliver us...*
> (2 Corinthians 1:8-10, emphasis mine)

Paul said that he and his companions were under such enormous pressure that it was *far beyond* their ability to endure. This doesn't sound like "God won't give you more than you can handle" to me. Here's the catch though. Paul gives the reason for their despair. *"But this happened that we might not rely on ourselves but on God,"* who, by the way, is so powerful that He can raise the dead.

Peter tells us to "Humble yourselves, therefore, under God's mighty hand, that He may lift you up [*promise to take care of you*] in due time [*in His timing*]. *Cast all your anxiety on Him* because He cares for you" (1 Peter 5:6-7, emphasis mine). I read a devotional by John Piper a long time ago on this particular verse that has stuck with me all these years. He was explaining that one way to humble ourselves is to give all our anxieties to God. This means that one hindrance to giving Him our anxieties is pride, and we all know that pride is sin. It is an affront to God, and undue worry is a form of pride. Simply put: our pride is a form of unbelief and does not like to trust God for His future grace. On the other hand, "faith [humility] admits the need for help. Pride won't. Faith [humility] banks on God to give help. Pride won't. Faith [humility] casts anxieties on God. Pride won't." [6] Therefore, we must turn from self-reliance to God-reliance and put our faith in His all-sufficient power.

God *will* stretch us beyond our breaking point. He *will* take us beyond our own capacity to endure. His deepest desire is to have us fully, *100%*, relying on Him. God so desires our whole-hearted faith that He will, if necessary, take away all other securities on which we are tempted to rely on. He wants us to grow deeper in our faith and confidence that He is *all* we need. I can imagine that one of the most beautiful sounds to the ear of God is His children crying out to Him, "I need you!"

He wants us to be able to say as the psalmist, Asaph, did, "Whom have I in heaven but you? And earth has nothing I desire besides you. My flesh and my heart may fail, but God is the strength of my heart and my portion forever" (Psalm 73:25-26); and as David did when he said, "Some trust in chariots and some in horses, but we trust in the name of the Lord our God" (Psalm 20:7).

Refined by Fire

The Bible often refers to two different types of fire. One is the fire of God's judgment. The other is the fire that refines and purifies His people. The former is promised for those who refuse Him. The latter, though painful, is not only promised but necessary for the true-born child of God. The refining process for gold and silver is to achieve perfection, and to remove all the impurities that exist within these metals. So it is for us also. I heard the following story once that speaks to this so well.

> A young man happened upon a silversmith who refined silver and gold from raw materials, sitting in front of his fire. "Why do you heat the metal?" he asked?
>
> The Refiner answered, "In order to make precious silver I have to remove all the impurities that make it worth *less* than it really is." The young man thought about his own life and how one time of fiery suffering or another was required to remove some of the 'junk' in his own life.
>
> "Why do you sit while you work?", inquired the visitor.
>
> The Refiner replied, "I have to watch the fire closely. Too little heat and the impurities will not be removed; too much heat and the precious metal will be destroyed and made worthless." The young man reflected on how his life of comfort

had brought a sense of complacency that led him to abandon his dreams, settling instead for a humdrum life. But he had also come through painful fiery times with character and strength that he would not have found elsewhere.

Then the young man asked The Refiner, "How do you know when the silver is at the right temperature?"

The Refiner smiled and answered, "I know the purifying is complete when I can see my reflection in the silver." The young man marveled at the answer thinking, "That is true in my life. My own fiery trials will only be complete when *My Refiner's image* can be seen in me."

We all have aspects of our own lives that need to be transformed by The Refiner: our selfish desires, ambitions, and time-wasting activities; our tendencies to quickly judge others and gossip behind their backs; our inklings to be envious, spiteful, and resentful; our pride that seeks recognition and honor. God is the only one who is able to free us from these impurities and transform us into the likeness of Christ and into a people worthy of His calling. And He will use whatever means He deems necessary to accomplish this end goal.

Paul tells us that he was given a "thorn in his flesh" to keep him from being conceited (2 Corinthians 12:7). Joseph was haughty, flaunting his dreams about being exalted to such a high status that even his family would be bowing down to him. God took Joseph through the furnace of affliction in the land of Egypt to kill his pride. It feels extreme, doesn't it? However, God deemed it necessary for Joseph so he could become the humble servant God wanted to use to "save many lives" (Genesis 50:19-20). As we read in the first chapter, King Nebuchadnezzar learned a thing or two about humility also. In fact, there is a whole chapter in the book of Daniel that he wrote himself about his wrestling with pride and how God brought him to his knees in humility before Him. King Nebuchadnezzar speaks of the Lord after his lesson: "Now I, Nebuchadnezzar, praise and exalt and glorify the King of heaven, because everything He does is right and all His ways are just. And *those who walk in pride He is able to humble*" (Daniel 4:37, emphasis mine).

Here are a few more verses that illustrate how God uses our burdens to test our hearts and refine our faith. However, as I've stated before, remember that these biblical authors, while writing under the inspiration of the Holy Spirit, never seemed to have a problem with assigning our suffering to God.

Remember how the Lord your God led you all the way
in the wilderness these forty years, *to humble and
test you in order to know what was in your heart*,
whether or not you would keep His commands.
(Deuteronomy 8:2, emphasis mine)

But He knows the way that I take;
when He has tested me, I will come forth as gold.
(Job 23:10, emphasis mine)

*For you, God, tested us; You refined us like silver.
You brought us into prison and laid burdens on our backs.*
You let people ride over our heads; *we went through
fire and water*, but You brought us to a place of abundance.
(Psalm 66:10-12, emphasis mine)

The crucible is for silver, and the furnace
is for gold, and *the Lord tests hearts*.
(Proverbs 17, ESV, emphasis mine)

Behold, I have refined you, but not as silver;
I have tried you in the furnace of affliction.
(Isaiah 48:10, ESV, emphasis mine)

And *I will put [them] into the fire, and refine them*
as one refines silver, and test them as gold is tested.
They will call upon my name, and I will answer them. I will say,
'They are my people'; and they will say, 'The Lord is my God.'
(Zechariah 13:9, ESV, emphasis mine)

Conclusion

Our sanctification is part of our redemption process. It is the vehicle which transports us from the start line to the finish line. Grace is a gift. Suffering is a gift. Both of these gifts work together to deliver us to the ultimate gift: sharing in Christ's glory for all eternity.

God is our Master Gardener. He prunes us by cutting off the *bad fruit* and *deadwood* in our lives. He is our Refiner who uses His fire to reveal our sin and He is intentional to rid us of it. He has an end goal: to conform us to the likeness of Christ (Romans 8:29), and He uses our adversity as the means to get us there. And He knows exactly what each one of us needs to bring about this end result.

The world cannot understand this type of refining. The means by which God uses to grow us are simply not perceivable to the world. The objective of the world is to avoid pain, difficulties, and uncomfortable situations, so they can't understand the idea that pain can be used for our good. But our sovereign and loving Father allows us to know affliction because it is, as Peter says, creating in us something more valuable than gold: our faith (1 Peter 1:7). He's not concerned with our comfort. He's concerned with our conformity.

'Tis my happiness below
Not to live without the cross,
But the Savior's power to know,
Sanctifying every loss;

Trials must and will befall,
But with humble faith to see
Love inscribed upon them all,
This is happiness to me.

God, in Israel, sows the seeds,
Of affliction, pain and toil;
These spring up, and choke the weeds
Which would else o'erspread the soil;

Trials make the promise sweet,
Trials give new life to prayer;
Trials bring me to His feet,
Lay me low, and keep me there. [7]

———————— •♦♦♦♦• ————————

May God Himself, the God of peace, sanctify you through and through.
May your whole spirit, soul and body be kept blameless at the coming of our
Lord Jesus Christ. The one who calls you is faithful, and He will do it.

1 THESSALONIANS 5:23-24

The Gift of Discipline

When God says, 'I will not leave you alone', He is not only promising His continuing presence, He is promising you Holy confrontation when we abandon Him. [1]

- Bryan Chapell

When I started formulating the outline for this book, our third *why, The Gift of Discipline,* was set to be its own chapter. However, when I sat down to begin writing, (unknowingly, or maybe in unconscious denial) I began feeling uneasy and exposed. I'm sure you can probably sympathize with the fact that the topic of God's discipline isn't really all that popular and can make people uncomfortable, so I tried to come up with ways to quietly slip it in at the end of our last chapter. Talking about being sanctified by refining and pruning is so much more comfortable than by way of discipline. God's discipline is just another form of refining and pruning, right? Well, wrong actually. Therefore, I couldn't stop wrestling with it. I slowly began to admit to myself that the problem was me. I didn't want to be vulnerable as I recalled the painful discipline God has used to bring rebuke and correction into my own life.

Although discipline is used to make us holy and conform us to His Son's image, in truth, it really isn't used as a means of sanctification in the same way testing, refining, and pruning is. Where our testing and refining help to remove our fleshly desires and attitudes and strengthen our faith, discipline is used to confront blatant sin in our lives. I love Bryan Chapell's quote at the beginning of the chapter because I think it expresses the purpose of discipline in the best possible way. It is God's promise, as our loving Father, to bring us, His children, into a "holy confrontation when we abandon Him." Rightly so. As His children, our blatant sin must be confronted. It is used to turn us around, correct us, and restore our relationship with our Maker.

Discipline vs. Punishment

Before fully diving into this chapter though, I need to make the distinction between discipline and punishment. I've heard too many Christians say that they've felt like God was punishing them for their sins. To be honest, I've even felt this way at times. But let's take a close look at what punishment really means and how it is different from the discipline I'm talking about. Punishment is designed to implement a penalty for misconduct. It's asserting justice or avenging a wrong. Discipline, on the other hand, is used for correction, reproof, and admonishment.

If we are in Christ, then the punishment for our sin was laid upon Him (Isaiah 53:5). Jesus took our punishment — the full wrath of God poured out for our sin. He satisfied God's justice and full payment was accepted. God, therefore, cannot demand punishment for our sin again. However, though every sin is forgiven in Christ, God's discipline is designed to confront us and to bring us back into repentance each time we do something that offends the Holy God we serve. Samuel Bolton once said:

> That which the believer suffers for sin is not penal,
> arising from vindictive justice, but medicinal,
> arising from a fatherly love. It is His medicine,
> not His punishment; His chastisement, not His
> sentence; His correction, not His condemnation. [2]

God Faithfulness in Discipline

Because God's love for His children is so extravagant, He determines to be faithful in His promise of discipline. Moses and David both experienced God's faithful discipline in their lives. In Psalm 119:75, David says, "...in faithfulness you have afflicted me." And in Psalm 90:8 Moses states, "You have set our iniquities before you, our secret sins in the light of your presence." If we are truly His, we need to be ready for God's faithfulness to confront us and convict us of our own sin. Moreover, we should desire it!

Time and again we see God's hand of discipline upon His chosen people, Israel, when they would turn away from Him and follow after other gods. For more than 800 years, they continued in a painful cycle of falling into sinful disobedience, experiencing God's discipline, and eventually repenting and returning to God. But after so many cycles and after countless Judges and Prophets sent by God continuing to warn them of His impending judgment because of their unrepentant sin and wickedness, He finally told them He was going to rip them from their land (2 Kings 17:18-20; 2 Chronicles 36:15-20). In 722 BC, the Assyrians destroyed Israel (the Northern Kingdom) and took their people into exile. Then in 586 BC, Judah (the Southern Kingdom in Jerusalem) was destroyed by Babylon, and the survivors were exiled to Babylon for seventy years.

The book of Lamentations was written by the prophet Jeremiah. It is the recording of his lamenting over the promised destruction of Jerusalem, which he himself prophesied and recorded in the book of Jeremiah. In his lamenting, Jeremiah writes, *"Because of the LORD's great love we are not consumed*, for His compassions never fail. They are new every morning; *great is your faithfulness*" (Lamentations 3:22-23, emphasis mine). Jeremiah was feeling pretty consumed with grief as he wrote these words, yet he was still reminded of God's love and compassion. And because God allowed a remnant to survive and go into exile, Jeremiah speaks of God's mercy. I have to think, as he was looking out over the destruction, Jeremiah was being reminded not only of God's faithfulness to His people and His promises, but also His faithfulness to follow through with His discipline.

Nevertheless, 2 Chronicles 36 ends with a promise of hope. The Israelites would return to their land and rebuild the temple (2 Chronicles. 36:21-23). And as a result of God's discipline, the people experienced tremendous spiritual growth during the 70 years of their captivity. Without having access to their temple, the Israelites learned that obedience was better than sacrifice (1 Samuel 15:22). In the end, God's discipline strengthened His people and restored their faith. After returning from Babylon with a renewed focus on being faithful to God (Ezra 9:10-15), they rebuilt the temple and did not resume their corrupt and sinful worship of Baal.

Discipline from Fatherly Love

> *It is never said, "Whom the Lord loveth He enricheth,"*
> *but it is said, "Whom the Lord loveth He chasteneth."* [3]
>
> *- Charles Spurgeon*

At the moment of our salvation we are told that God accepts us as His children. He adopts us into His family and we become co-heirs with Christ (Romans 8:15-17). God is a Good Father who has vowed to protect and provide for His children (Deuteronomy 33:3,26-29). Matthew tells us that our Father in heaven gives good gifts (Matthew 7:11). Luke, in his gospel, says it this way: If we, as sinful man, can give good gifts to our children, "how much more will [our] Heavenly Father give the Holy Spirit to those who ask Him?" (Luke 11:13). James, the brother of Jesus, tells us that "every good gift and every perfect gift is from above, coming down from the Father of Lights" (James 1:17). And lastly, we know from the author of Hebrews that God, the Father, disciplines those He loves (Hebrews 12:5-7).

I know that some of you reading this book may have never known the true love of a father. Any discipline (if you can even call it that) you did receive was probably inflicted out of retribution and ill will, to demean and criticize. I can understand how this can affect your view of God as a loving Father, especially when it comes to His discipline. However, only true love will proceed fatherly discipline, and the goal will always be to bring gentle restoration back to the relationship.

I have found in my own parenting experience that a child who is disciplined out of love feels more secure and affirmed overall. They have a better relationship with their parents as a whole, and feel loved even when they are being disciplined for making bad choices.

As children, when my kids misbehaved (i.e.: throw a game controller at the head of their sibling), in the moment they were often unable to recognize that what they did was wrong. All they could see was how they were wronged. And in their eyes, this justified their misbehavior, therefore not welcoming the discipline. It wasn't until later, after the discipline, that they recognized their grievances and changed their behavior.

We as Christians often do this ourselves. When we blatantly sin, I would venture to say we are usually very aware of it. However, while in sin, we often begin making excuses as to why we are justified in behaving the way we are. It takes the rod of our Father's discipline before we can recognize our grievances, but once we finally see our sin through the eyes of a Holy God, we then welcome the correction, knowing it comes from a place of love.

I believe we often think that God's love and kindness is

inconsistent with His discipline. Perhaps it is because we cannot appreciate how seriously God loves us. He is determined in doing us good, even if it involves pain. He doesn't willingly bring the affliction (Lamentations 3:32-33). He takes no delight in seeing us suffer under His discipline. However, He knows it will bring us to the conformity of His own image so we will be fit to dwell in His presence.

King Hezekiah accepted the Lord's discipline, knowing it came from a place of love to keep him from destruction.

> Surely it was for my benefit that I suffered such anguish.
> *In your love you kept me from* the pit of *destruction*;
> you have put all my sins behind your back.
> (Isaiah 38:17, emphasis mine)

Jesus tells the Laodicean Church, "Those whom I love I rebuke and discipline. So be earnest and repent" (Revelation 3:19). Paul tells us that God's kindness leads to repentance (Romans 2:4). This is the kindest and most loving thing our Father can do for us. God wants us to rest in our salvation and repentance is the only way to find it (Isaiah 30:15).

William Gurnall, an Anglican clergyman who preached during the 1600's, said, "Sin's kisses kill; God's wounds cure." I would so much more prefer God's discipline than His wrath on my sin. How sweet has His gracious, heavy hand been on my life. Just like my own children knew that I loved them when I disciplined them, I know that I am loved because my Father disciplines me. The author of Hebrews assures us that His discipline is evidence of His love:

> And have you completely forgotten this word of encouragement that addresses you as a father addresses his son? It says, "My son, do not make light of the Lord's discipline, and do not lose heart when He rebukes you, because *the Lord disciplines*

the one He loves, and He chastens everyone He accepts as His Son." Endure hardship as discipline; God is treating you as His children. For what children are not disciplined by their father? If you are not disciplined – and everyone undergoes discipline – then you are not legitimate, not true sons and daughters at all. Moreover, we have all had human fathers who disciplined us and we respected them for it. How much more should we submit to the Father of spirits and live! They disciplined us for a little while as they thought best; *but God disciplines us for our good,* in order *that we may share in His holiness.* No *discipline seems pleasant at the time, but painful.* Later on, however, *it produces a harvest of righteousness and peace* for those *who have been trained by it.* (Hebrews 12:5-11, emphasis mine)

In the 7th chapter of 2 Samuel we find God establishing His covenant with David. Within this promise, He tells David that his son, Solomon, will proceed his throne; more importantly that God's fatherly love and discipline was promised to guide Solomon. God says:

When your days are over and you rest with your ancestors, I will raise up your offspring to succeed you, your own flesh and blood, and I will establish his kingdom. He is the one who will build a house for my Name, and I will establish the throne of his kingdom forever. *I will be his Father, and he will be my son. When he does wrong, I will punish him with a rod wielded by men, with floggings inflicted by human hands. But my love will never be taken away from him...* (2 Samuel 7:14-15, emphasis mine).

As king, some years later, Solomon writes these words of wisdom:

My son, *do not despise the Lord's discipline*,
and do not resent His rebuke, because
the Lord disciplines those He loves,
as a father the son he delights in.
(Proverbs 3:11–12, emphasis mine)

David knew all too well the discipline of the Lord in his own life. The lesson we can take from him is that he recognized it as God's hand of mercy upon him and that His love would never be taken away from him. Therefore, he counted it as joy.

For His anger lasts only for a moment,
but *His favor lasts a lifetime.*
(Psalm 30:5, emphasis mine)

Blessed is the one you discipline,
Lord, the one you teach from your law.
(Psalm 94:12, emphasis mine)

It was *good for me to be afflicted* so
that I might learn your decrees.
(Psalm 119:71, emphasis mine)

Let me hear joy and gladness; let *the bones
you have crushed rejoice*. Hide your face from
my sins and blot out all my iniquity.
(Psalm 51:8-9, emphasis mine)

This last verse is found in the middle of Psalm 51, which is a psalm of David's confession after committing adultery with Bathsheba. God used the prophet, Nathan, to expose David's sin.

Because David was a man after God's heart, he understood that this rebuke came from love. There was always a consequence carried out for David's sin, however, he was always ready to acknowledge it, repent of it, and allow himself to fall into the hands of God. He knew the heart of God was to restore their relationship, to forgive and show mercy because he was loved by God.

Oh, how many times the Lord has done this same thing for me! I am undeserving of His grace, yet He continues to extend it. Therefore, I am undone by His love for me. Each time the Lord has confronted me for my own blatant sin, the weight of it (knowing I've offended the holy God whom I claim to serve) has been so heavy to the point of feeling crushed, yet so sweet to my soul at the same time. Though I am unworthy, He continues to pursue me. Though I fail Him, He is always faithful. Out of His loving kindness, He confronts, disciplines, and restores me. It is better by far to fall into the hands of a holy, yet compassionate God, than to be left to my own demise and the wickedness of my own heart.

David says it best (doesn't he always?) in this beautiful psalm:

> *The Lord is compassionate and gracious, slow to anger, abounding in love.* He will not always accuse, nor will He harbor His anger forever; *He does not treat us as our sins deserve or repay us according to our iniquities.* For as high as the heavens are above the earth, *so great is His love for those who fear Him; as far as the east is from the west, so far has He removed our transgressions from us. As a father has compassion on his children, so the Lord has compassion on those who fear Him;* for He knows how we are formed, He remembers that we are dust. (Psalm 103:8–14, emphasis mine)

Conclusion

God holds two rods. One is fashioned for His Fatherly kindness and love to correct His children, the other is for His wrath and justice toward His enemies. For the Christian, Jesus took the rod of His wrath in our place. We have been forgiven and have been adopted into the family of God (Romans 8:14-17). However, now that we are in His family, as sons and daughters we will receive our Father's rod of correction. Yet His motive is always love because He understands the consequences of sin far better than we do. May we learn not to despise His discipline, but rather be encouraged by it.

> *Oh, to grace how great a debtor*
> *Daily I'm constrained to be*
> *Let Thy goodness like a fetter*
> *Bind my wandering heart to Thee*
>
> *Prone to wander, Lord I feel it*
> *Prone to leave the God I love*
> *Here's my heart, oh take and seal it*
> *Seal it for Thy courts above* [4]

————————— ✦✦✦✦✦ —————————

Lord, do not remove your hand of discipline from me, for it is life, but discipline me in your loving kindness and grace. May I accept the blessing of your rebuke and stern hand as my loving Father who desires our restored relationship. Although it is painful, I know it is profitable. Turn me from my rebellious ways and conform me into your image. I pray as David prayed, "Have mercy on me, O God, according to your unfailing love…let the bones you have crushed rejoice…Create in me a pure heart, O God, and renew a steadfast spirit within me. Do not cast me from your presence or take your Holy Spirit from me. Restore to me the joy of your salvation and grant me a willing spirit, to sustain me" (Psalm 51:1,8,10-12).

The Gift of Comfort

Empathy flows not from the causes of pain,
but from the company of pain. And we are all in it together. [1]

- John Piper

So far, with the first three *whys* (gifts) of our suffering, our Biblical lens has been focused on us. We have been the center of attention. However, for the next three *whys* we will take the attention off of ourselves and begin to focus our lens outward. Sometimes we get so wrapped up in our own little world, and so focused on our own pain and suffering, that we forget to look up and acknowledge the suffering world around us. Have you ever had to be reminded that it's not all about you? Well, it's true. And I've probably needed reminding of this a little too often. It isn't easy to stay outwardly focused when dealing with your own mental, emotional, and physical pain. Nevertheless, God has not just promised to use our own suffering for our sanctification and discipline, but He is also actively and simultaneously using it to affect the world around us.

God created us with the need for relationship. After all, He is a relational God and we are made in His image. Above all, He desires our first affections and wants our full devotion. In our hearts, no one is to be loved more than Him. This is His first commandment: "Love the Lord your God with all your heart and with all your soul and with all your mind" (Matthew 22:37-40). However, His next command is to love our neighbor as much as we love ourselves. So how do we do this? In part, it is walking with them through their own suffering. However, before we can effectively use our suffering to help others, we must have a well to draw from. We must first receive comfort from God before we can give the same comfort to others.

Finding Christ's Comfort in our Suffering

You don't have to be alone in your hurt! Comfort is yours…it's all been made possible by your Savior. He went without comfort so you might have it. He postponed joy so you might share in it. He willingly chose isolation so you might never be alone in your hurt and sorrow. [2]

-Joni Eareckson Tada

God desires us to seek His comfort above all others. He knows that anything outside of Himself will be fleeting, and because His well will never run dry, we should always approach God's throne of grace, above all else, in our time of need. A side benefit of Jesus' sacrificial suffering is His ability to comfort us and empathize with us in our weakness.

For ***we do not have a high priest who is unable to empathize with our weaknesses***, but we have one who has been tempted in every way, just as we are - yet He did not sin. ***Let us then approach God's throne of grace with confidence, so that we may receive mercy and***

find grace to help us in our time of need.
(Hebrews 4:15–16, emphasis mine)

Praise be to the God and Father of our Lord Jesus Christ,
the Father of compassion and the *God of all comfort,*
who comforts us in all our troubles... For just as we share
abundantly in the sufferings of Christ, so also *our*
comfort abounds through Christ.
(2 Corinthians 1:3–5, emphasis mine)

John chapter 17 is one of the most comforting passages in scripture. It's a record of Jesus praying to His Father while celebrating the Passover with His disciples on the night of His betrayal. During their time together, Jesus spent His last hours teaching, encouraging, and instructing them on what was about to happen and what was to come. Chapters 13-17 are often referred to as *The Upper Room Discourse.* At the end of His time with them, Jesus begins to pray for His disciples (chapter 17). It is a profound, heartfelt prayer that served as a reminder to His disciples of His deep love and concern for them. But He didn't just stop there. Jesus then began to pray for all believers. *ALL* believers; from that time, till now, and up to His return. That's you. That's me. He was praying for us!

My prayer is not for them alone [the disciples]. *I pray*
also for those who will believe in me through their
message... Father, I want those you have given
me to be with me where I am, and to see my glory.
(John 17:20,24, emphasis mine)

David, from his own understanding of being a shepherd, writes Psalm 23. Just as his sheep did not fear the dark valleys he took them through, he too is comforted by God's presence, as his Shepherd, through his own dark valleys.

> Even though I walk through the darkest valley,
> I will fear no evil, for you are with me;
> *your rod and your staff, they comfort me.*
> (Psalm 23:4, emphasis mine)

Comforting and Strengthening Each Other Through our Suffering

Not only can we draw our comfort from the examples we see above in Jesus' prayer and through the psalms of David, but we can also draw from the trials, betrayals, torments, persecutions, and sufferings of other godly men and women who we read about in the Bible. Each one of them endured their suffering, drawing on the comfort of God for themselves. Then, as with those who have come before us, like a domino effect, the trials we suffer are preparing us for the encouragement and solace of others.

Adding to his statement about being comforted by God (1 Corinthians 1:3-5, quoted above), Paul continues to expound on how his suffering is not only for the comfort of others, but also for their encouragement and progression of their faith.

> *If we are distressed, it is for your comfort* and salvation;
> *if we are comforted, it is for your comfort, which produces*
> *in you patient endurance* of the same sufferings we suffer.
> And our hope for you is firm, because we know
> that just as you share in our sufferings,
> *so also you share in our comfort.*
> (2 Corinthians 1:6-7, emphasis mine)

Paul is not only wanting to communicate that he and his companions are suffering on behalf of the comfort and faith of his converts, but he also encourages these new believers to do the same for each other.

Rejoice with those who rejoice; *mourn with those who mourn*.
(Romans 12:15, emphasis mine)

Carry each other's burdens, and in
this way you will fulfill the law of Christ.
(Galatians 6:2, emphasis mine)

Therefore, *encourage one another and build each other up*.
(1 Thessalonians 5:11, emphasis mine)

I recently read a secular article titled "How Comforting Others Helps You with Your Own Struggles" found in the *Greater Good Magazine*. Two studies were conducted that showed how helping other people through their struggles also helps with your own. The author of the article writes:

> Both studies point to the same answer: the skill of perspective-taking, which is the ability to put ourselves in someone else's shoes.... suggests that getting out of our heads and into the heads of others—empathy, in other words—is good for everyone involved. And when we feel alone in our suffering, we can turn to others both for our own sake and for theirs. [3]

I cite this article only for the Biblical principle behind it. (Actually, anytime I see science unknowingly backing up biblical truths, it makes me laugh. God's fingerprints are all around us, aren't they?) It was a good article on a topic that the Bible has already given credence to, and I'm guessing that you've already picked up on it. As our opening quote expresses, we need each other. Long before the above article was written, Solomon penned "As iron sharpens iron, so one person sharpens another" (Proverbs

27:17). The writer of Hebrews also tells us to "consider how we may spur one another on toward love and good deeds" (Hebrews 10:24).

We all have experienced some type of suffering, be it in the form of physical pain, mental anguish, or emotional distress at one time or another. Maybe you, like a couple friends of mine, have survived a horrible car accident that has forever changed your life; or like others I know, have experienced a house fire that has taken everything you've owned. Some of you have endured physical, verbal, and emotional abuse inflicted by someone you thought could be trusted. I think we have all had shattered dreams and failures. Like so many, maybe the loss of a job or the economy crashing has put you in financial distress. Maybe you have been in chronic pain and have ailments that have yet to be diagnosed that leaves you dependent on other people for your care; or maybe you're like my husband who has had to step into the roll as this caregiver. Maybe it's PTSD from some sort of trauma. Maybe you've lost a child, or have had multiple miscarriages, or have struggled with infertility. Maybe you're the mother who struggles with finding the patience and means to take care of a child with special needs; or you've felt like your reserves to battle postpartum depression have been depleted and you see no end in sight.

Whatever it is we have suffered, or are suffering, there is someone else who is going through the same trials who needs our comfort and support, and vice versa. Paul tells us, as the body of Christ, we "should have equal concern for each other. If one part suffers, every part suffers with it..." (1 Corinthians 12:25).

Just a couple days before starting this chapter I was speaking with a friend about this very topic. She was telling me about the suffering she had to endure from watching her two sons battle with the evils of addiction (praise God, they have since been freed). But while I can pray for and mourn with a mother who is going through the same ordeal with their loved one, my friend can offer the wisdom and understanding that she has obtained through her own journey. Prayer and compassion from people who haven't walked in our shoes are good, but encouraging, supporting, and comforting someone out of our personal experience is a ministry. My friend and I can have sympathy for one another and pray for each other (which we do), but I am better equipped to minister to someone who deals with chronic pain and depression from an incurable disease, just like she is better equipped to minister to another who is watching their family being devastated by addiction.

However, if we are given the opportunity to minister to someone whose shoes we have never walked in, even though we may not be able to speak to their present circumstances, we can always encourage and comfort them by pointing them back to three very important promises we find in Scripture: the promise of Christ's presence, the promise that their suffering is not wasted, and the sacrifice He made to secure their future hope. And when they have finished their own race, God will be faithful to welcome them into His kingdom where there will be no more tears, no more suffering, and no more pain (Revelation 21:4). This is the best thing we can do for someone who is needing our comfort.

Now, before we move on, I need to make one thing very clear. As Christians, we should never try to find advice from our friends who are outside of Christ and His body of believers. Unfortunately, I have made this mistake a time or two. Going to our non-believing friends can often invoke more bad decisions which can often lead to even more heartache. We are called to reach *out to* the world, but we are never called to reach *for* the world. However, with that said, I am by no means saying it's wrong to see a doctor or psychiatrist for severe depression or other mental health reasons. I would only warn to make sure whatever they are telling you does not contradict the Word of God.

Peter's Ministry

Simon Peter is another good example of how God uses us to comfort those around us. During the Last Supper, Jesus looks at Peter and point blank says to him, "Simon, Simon, behold, Satan demanded to have you, that he might sift you like wheat, but I have prayed for you that your faith may not fail. And when you have turned again, strengthen your brothers" (Luke 22:31-32, ESV).

There are three segments to this pronouncement Jesus gave to Peter that I would like to break down. The first two are a little off-topic, but I still think it will be beneficial for us in the long run. The first one is His statement about Satan sifting Peter. The second one is about Jesus praying for Peter. And the third (which is more relative to our topic) is about Peter strengthening his brothers.

➤ **Satan's Sifting:**

Pay attention to the language Jesus uses when He tells Peter about Satan's contribution in this narrative. He tells Peter that Satan *demanded* to have him so he could *sift him like wheat*. We know that to sift wheat means to separate the grain from the chaff. Sifting can also be related to refining. Does this ring a bell? Remember chapter 3 that talks about sanctification through a similar process? Up to this point in the book, we've only looked at how God uses our suffering, acting through His sovereign will, for our good. However, here it sounds as though Satan is responsible for the sifting of Peter. But is he really?

There are a few places in scripture that specifically give Satan the credit for being a messenger of pain, or playing a prominent role in causing calamity or inciting temptation in the lives of God's people (Genesis 3:1-6; 1 Chronicles 21:1; Job 1:6-12, 2:1-7, 2 Corinthians 12:7 are the ones I know about). So far, at the risk of losing popularity points, I have only cited scriptures that shine the spotlight on God taking credit for the suffering in the lives of His believers (again, not capriciously or arbitrarily, but only out of Fatherly love and kindness). However, what I want to highlight right now is that even though Satan is given the spotlight at times, he is still under the Sovereign hand of God. First, Satan must have permission to interfere with God's people. The NASB says that Satan "demanded *permission*" to sift Peter. Nonetheless, God didn't give Satan permission just *because* he demanded it. God doesn't have to give permission to anyone for anything, especially when it's demanded, and especially by Satan. Second, Satan cannot go beyond what God has allowed. God set boundaries on Peter's life, just as we see Him doing in the lives of Job (Job 1:12; 2:6) and King Nebuchadnezzar (Daniel 4:15,23). After telling Peter that Satan would sift him, Jesus declares the promise of Peter's restoration. Restoration infers boundaries. I like what John Piper says about this:

> Behind all disease and disability is the ultimate will of God. Not that Satan is not involved — he is probably always involved in one way or another with destructive purposes (Acts 10:38). But his power is not decisive. He cannot act without God's permission.[4]

Though some have tried, I cannot (nor ever will) make an argument for how God's sovereignty, Satan's power, along with man's free will and moral responsibilities all work together. In all the attempted explanations I've heard, one of these three components always ends up being left out, severely diminished, or completely overinflated. But here's the thing. Even though the Bible claims all three of these components, it never makes any effort to expound upon their association. It's one of the several mysteries about God that we will never fully understand. Remember Deuteronomy 29:29? "The secret things belong to the Lord our God, but the things revealed belong to us..." So in light of this, let's look at three things that scripture does reveal to us:

1. We have free will according to our sin nature (Romans 7:19).
2. Satan is working in the background (Ephesians 6:11-12).
3. But above all, God is Sovereign over *everything* (refer back to chapter 1).

What scripture does not reveal is *how* they all work cohesively together. So it is at this junction we just need to allow the Bible to speak for itself, lay down our pride, and submit to the authority of scripture.

> ### Jesus Praying

Let's start again by reading the whole portion of this scripture, but this time let's read it in the NASB version. Luke 22: 31-32 says:

> Simon, Simon, behold, Satan has demanded *permission* to sift you like wheat; ***but I have prayed for you, that your faith may not fail;*** and you, when once you have turned again, strengthen your brothers. (emphasis mine)

After such a shocking statement about Satan sifting him, Jesus encourages Peter. Remember the comfort we can find in Jesus' prayer for us in John chapter 17? Here Jesus is reminding Peter of the prayer He just prayed for him. He asked His Father to "protect them [Peter] from the evil one" (John 17:15).

The disciples believed in God's sovereignty. It alone was their reason and encouragement to pray, as it should be ours. If we believe He is able to answer our prayers, it is because we believe in His sovereignty. Why else would we pray? I think Jerry Bridges says it best this way:

> Prayer assumes the sovereignty of God. If God is not sovereign, we have no assurance that He is able to answer our prayers. Our prayers would become

nothing more than wishes. But while God's sovereignty, along with His wisdom and love, is the foundation of our trust in Him, prayer is the expression of that trust. [5]

Even so, we are talking about Jesus being the one praying here, not us or His disciples. When we pray, we cannot assume that God will grant all of our prayers all of the time. However, when Jesus, the sovereign Son of the Sovereign Father, prays to God on our behalf, how much more can we be assured and comforted by knowing that His prayers will *always* be answered. God is accountable to answering His Son's prayers. Why? Because, unlike us, Jesus will never pray for something that is outside of God's will. How can anything else be more comforting?

➤ Peter's Strengthening

The last portion of Jesus' statement to Peter is exactly what this chapter is about: suffering for the comfort and strength of our fellow believers. Jesus calls Peter to strengthen his brothers (his fellow disciples) after he is restored. Peter suffers. Peter is comforted. Peter becomes the comforter. First, God gave Satan permission to incite Peter to deny Christ. He used him to break Peter's pride and self-reliance. Nonetheless, God then restored him and forgave him. Once their relationship was reestablished, God gave Peter the ministry of strengthening the faith of his brothers. Once again, John Piper says it so much better than I can:

> The strengthened becomes the strengthener.... Whenever God encourages your heart with the promise that in Satan's sifting, your faith will not fail, then take that encouragement and double your joy by using it to strengthen your brothers and

sisters — with the very strength with which you have been strengthened. [6]

Conclusion

There will be times when we feel alone in our pain and sorrow, but it is within these times we can find the comfort of our Savior. He has promised it to us. We find it in His word and know it through His grace and our future hope. This grace, strength, and comfort God gives to us will then be poured out on those around us, many of whom we may not even be aware of. Because the way we suffer speaks volumes to the people around us, imagine how different our suffering would look if we could see it as a calling.

Regardless of whether or not we can fully understand someone else's suffering, whether or not we've ever walked in their shoes, the most loving and comforting thing we can do is to point them to our Savior, who has promised that He will use their trials to accomplish His good and loving purposes in their lives. We can bring them to the comfort Christ gives, the gift of their own suffering (Philippians 1:29 — our bedrock verse), and the gift of eternal salvation which He secured by way of His own suffering.

Being part of the body of Christ means we are all in this together. We need each other's comfort, but our first comfort should come from God. He comforts us so we may be comforted. By such, we, the comforted, now can become the comforters.

————— ✦✦✦✦✦ —————

May the God who gives endurance and encouragement give you the same attitude of mind toward each other that Christ Jesus had, so that with one mind and one voice you may glorify the God and Father of our Lord Jesus Christ.

ROMANS 15:5-6

The Gift of the Gospel

To suffer for the name of Christ is a two-sided equation.
The name of Christ is the cause of our added suffering, but the name
of Christ also becomes the purpose of our suffering. As cause, we can
expect to suffer for the name of Christ. As purpose, we can expect to
suffer, so that in our suffering we might testify to the name of Christ. [1]

~ Tony Reinke

lthough I put this *why*, *The Gift of the Gospel*, fifth in order, by no means is it intended to diminish its importance. In fact, I would venture to say it is the most important one so far, because everything starts here: the Gospel — the good news that Jesus Christ came to save the lost. The gospel is where true life begins for every believer. Without it, we would still be dead in our sin (Ephesians 2:1-3), and separated from God (Genesis 1:23; Isaiah 59:2; Ephesians 2:12).

As believers who have been born again by the Spirit, we have been given the gift of the gospel working its effect in us (1 Corinthians 15:10). But the gospel goes far beyond each one of us. We are set apart *from* the world, *for* the world. We are called away from the world so we can reach our world. This calling away is initiated by God through the workings of His Spirit (Philippians 1:19; 2:13; 3:3), so we can reach the unbelieving world. God does the saving and the sanctifying, but in some unexplainable, glorious way He has given us a part in the process.

Our Ministry of Reconciliation

All this is from God, who reconciled us to Himself through Christ and gave us the ministry of reconciliation: that God was reconciling the world to Himself in Christ, not counting people's sins against them. And He has committed to us the message of reconciliation. We are therefore Christ's ambassadors, as though God were making His appeal through us. We implore you on Christ's behalf: Be reconciled to God.

2 Corinthians 5:18-20

In the Great Commission, before ascending to heaven Jesus told His disciples, "All authority in heaven and on earth has been given to me. *Therefore* go and make disciples of all nations, baptizing them in the name of the Father and of the Son and of the Holy Spirit, and teaching them to obey everything I have commanded you" (Matthew 28:19-20, emphasis mine). By His authority, Jesus commissioned His disciples with the task of testifying to God's mercy and grace which had been poured out to the world through the events of His death, burial, and resurrection.

Paul tells the church of Corinth, "For what I received I passed on to you as of first importance: that Christ died for our sins according to the Scriptures, that He was buried, that He was raised on the third day according to the Scriptures..." (1 Corinthians 15:3-4). This gospel message that was passed down to Paul is the same gospel message Jesus commissioned His disciples to spread. Paul was just one of the links in the chain. From the beginning, this was how

God planned to get His message out. Every disciple made would in turn make more disciples.

> The faith and love that spring from the hope stored up for you in heaven and about which you have already heard in the true message of *the gospel* that *has come to you*. In the same way, *the gospel is bearing fruit and growing throughout the whole world – just as it has been doing among you since the day you heard it* and truly understood God's grace.
> (Colossians 1:5-6, emphasis mine)

> *You became imitators of us and of the Lord, for you welcomed the message* in the midst of severe suffering with the joy given by the Holy Spirit. *And so you became a model* to all the believers in Macedonia and Achaia.
> (1 Thessalonians 1:6-7, emphasis mine)

Just imagine if you could count all the disciples God used to carry the gospel, tracing them like a family tree, from that day till now — to you! I can't even begin to wrap my mind around that. But here's the thing: Jesus didn't need His disciples (and subsequently you and I) to evangelize the world. He could have chosen another way to spread His gospel. But He didn't. He chose fallible men and women to carry out the task. I still have yet to fully understand how or why God chose to expand His Kingdom this way, but it's like I used to tell my kids, we don't need to understand the whys before we obey. I will never understand why God chooses to use the foolish and finite to display His wisdom and splendor to a dying world (1 Corinthians 1:27-28), but we obey because we are commanded to *"Go therefore"*.

> *I have become its* [the gospel's] *servant by the commission God gave me* to present to you the word of God in its fullness.
> (Colossians 1:25, emphasis mine)

Our reconciliation is for the reconciliation of others. First God reconciles us to Himself (Colossians 1:22), then He makes us ambassadors for Christ, giving our own ministry of reconciliation: to make His appeal to the rest of the world to be reconciled to God. Richard Wurmbrand, in his book, *Tortured for Christ*, says, "Every soul won for Christ must be made to be a soul winner." [2]

Suffering For Our Mission Field

To suffer for the name of Christ is to be positioned firmly within the sovereign will of our Father, often for new gospel witness. [3]

~ Tony Reinke

Though our words are a fundamental necessity in our role as ambassadors for the gospel of Christ (Romans 10:14-15), ironically another fascinating contribution we have in spreading His message is through our suffering. God uses our pain and suffering to spread His goodness and glory to the lives around us. There will, of course, be times when our suffering is a direct result of sharing the gospel (in some places it is more prevalent and severe than others), but I will talk about that in the next section. In this section, however, I'm going to talk about how our personal trials and suffering can be used as a means by which we share the gospel.

God has given every single one of us a unique circle of influence, and if we are intentional about looking around us, we will find countless opportunities to shine the light of God's grace to the people within those circles. God has put us exactly where we need to be, when we are meant to be there, for the people who need to hear our message. This is our mission field. Don't think of a missionary as just the "called" one who goes to a mission field in another country. We are *all* called to be missionaries, first to our family, and second, to the world around us. It is by no mistake that you are where you are. Remember our verses from the first chapter about God's sovereignty?

> In their hearts humans plan their course,
> but *the LORD establishes their steps."*
> (Proverbs 16:9, emphasis mine)

> Many are the plans in a person's heart,
> but *it is the LORD's purpose that prevails.*
> (Proverbs 19:21, emphasis mine)

Both my husband and I were born and raised in Colorado. Our two children were born there as well. We had no intention, let alone ever conceived of the idea to leave our families, our friends, and our beloved home state. But God had another plan. And I won't lie, originally I did not like His plan.

We had been visiting Phil's family in Las Vegas over Labor Day weekend in 2001. One night, while staying with his dad, I felt like I had a wrestling match with God from sundown to sun up. When I laid down for bed that evening, I began to hear God speak to me, and I was *not* happy about it! I know some people think that God doesn't speak to people in direct ways, but there have been a few times in my life that I have clearly heard Him deep in my soul. Here is how I know it's Him speaking though and not my own thoughts: what my spirit hears never lines up with my desires. Not once have I liked what He's told me. And here, once again, that night my will was not in line with what God was telling me. But needless to say, after a long, sleep-deprived night, trying to tell Him "No!" and why He was wrong, my will was finally broken. I was still not thrilled with His plan; however, I finally rolled over at 6 am, woke Phil up, and told him something he would have never imagined coming out of my mouth. "You need to test for the Las Vegas fire department."

Here's a little backstory. Phil had grown up wanting to be a firefighter. It was his dream career. Me? I had always known that I *didn't* want to marry a firefighter. About a month after we started dating, he told me his plan to test for the Denver fire department. Well, I made sure he knew right up front, if that was his plan, he could do it without me. I think it goes without saying (thankfully) he chose me over his dream job. However, after 8 years of Phil sacrificing his dreams, putting me and our children above himself, God made it abundantly clear to me that it was my turn to make some sacrifices. (Oh, and did I tell you that I did *not* want to move to Las Vegas - of all places?)

I told God, that morning in September of 2001, if He was going to ask us to do something so ridiculous and outrageous, then it was going to be all on Him. And it was. As people like to say, "The rest is history." A little less than a year later we moved to Las Vegas and received the phone call. Phil was hired. Most people don't realize how unheard of it is to be hired by the first fire department someone ever applies to. At that time, it was like winning the lottery. The funny thing is, we were completely ignorant to this fact. Neither did we know that the Las Vegas fire department was one of the most difficult in the nation to get on at that time; and little did we know that when he applied, there were over 3,500 applicants for only 50 positions. I could write a small book detailing every miraculous turn of events — doors which no man could have opened — that landed Phil on the City of Las Vegas Fire and Rescue in August of the next year.

Our story is only one example. When God wants you somewhere, He will place you there. Sometimes we're ready and willing to go; sometimes we fight it. Often, we can end up somewhere we didn't even realize God had His hand in, thinking we were making up our own plans. But regardless of how it happens, we are always where we are supposed to be. It may not feel like it at times. It may not be permanent. No one can know God's plan and how He uses the circumstances in our lives to move us into position to be His hands and feet. Of all places, Phil and I would have never chosen to uproot our family and move to Nevada, or end up in Utah for that matter.

However, there have been countless times in the 19 years since moving from Colorado that God has given us opportunities to be His hands and feet, to be a light in the darkness for the people around us.

In the last chapter we talked about suffering for the comfort of the brethren — the church — but we also suffer for the unbeliever to bring him or her to Christ. Every one of us has been through something which God can use to open unseen doors for the good news of Christ to be shared. Have you ever found yourself in the company of your unbelieving neighbor or coworker who is going through the same thing you have gone through, or are going through? Someone who needs the light of Christ in their life? There are no coincidences. God has a plan to use every one of our struggles and perceived defeats for His victories. Through our suffering, God is making His appeal to the unbelievers around us to be reconciled to the only Savior who can give them the grace, peace, and hope they need through their own trials. Paul tells the church at Corinth that his distresses were for their salvation (2 Corinthians 1:6). So consider this for yourself: every time a personal tragedy or trial hits, it will always bring opportunities to advance His kingdom. Our best witness will always be in our worst circumstances.

Gospel Advancement Through Persecution

God intends for the afflictions of Christ to be presented to the world through the afflictions of his people. God really means for the body of Christ, the church, to experience some of the suffering he experienced so that when we proclaim the cross as the way to life, people will see the marks of the cross in us and feel the love of the cross from us. [4]

~ John Piper

I once had the glorious opportunity to lead a friend to Christ. As incredible as that experience was, I have to admit, I was surprised when I found some resentment directed my way, along with someone's attempt to malign my character. I was guilty of acting like what I would call a Disneyland Christian — someone who is caught up in the "magic" of naivety, delusional to the cost of being a Christian. As Christians here in America, we can often be tempted to think that it will be easy to share the gospel without getting any pushback. Peter makes sure to dispel any such notion to his readers. He tells them, "do not be surprised...as though something strange were happening to you. But rejoice...as you participate in the sufferings of Christ..." (1 Peter 4:12-13).

I'm still sad to say that even after all these years and after all that God has brought me through, it can still feel scary to open my mouth and share the gospel. Often, I find myself holding back because I feel my words are inadequate and I'm afraid of what they might think. Sometimes it's because I'm fearful that my relationship with that person might change. But it all comes down to this: how much do I love God and love my neighbor? The most loving thing I can do for them is to share the gospel, even if it means I am rebuked or reviled. Paul tells his disciples in Philippi to "conduct [themselves] in a manner worthy of the gospel...without being frightened...by those who oppose you" (Philippians 1:27-28).

Paul understood his mission; he comprehended the gravity of it. And moreover, he embraced the sheer fact that he was going to be persecuted for it. After all, his conversion happened while on his way to find and arrest more Christians in Damascus. If *he* was persecuting Christians because of the name of Christ, then it was a given that he too would be persecuted for the name of Christ. This is what God told Ananias, the disciple who was sent to heal Paul's blindness:

> Go! *This man* [Paul] *is my chosen instrument to proclaim my name* to the Gentiles and their kings and to the people of Israel. *I will show him how much he must suffer for my name.*
> (Act 9:15–16, emphasis mine)

Our persecution *because of* the gospel becomes an amplifier *for* the gospel. God's ultimate objective is to bring glory to His name, by way of His grace, through the sufferings of His Son. The Son then turns to His followers and tells them that they need to follow in His footsteps (Matthew 16:24). Now Paul tells us:

> *I fill up in my flesh what is still lacking in regard to Christ's afflictions*, for the sake of His body, which is the church.
> (Colossians 1:24, emphasis mine)

What did Paul mean when he said "I fill up my flesh what is still lacking in regard to Christ's affliction"? Well, God prepared a love offering for the world through His Son, Jesus, by suffering and dying for our sin, right? So what did Christ's afflictions accomplish? Our debt paid in full! *Nothing* can be added to complete this gift. His afflictions lack nothing except one thing: the representation of it.

Let's use Tchaikovsky for an example of representation. In 1892, this brilliant composer had composed one of the most famous ballets in the world, *The Nutcracker Suite*. The only reason this ballet has become so popular still to this day, is because there have been countless ballet companies that have continued to produce the ballet. Like a good story, it continues to be shared by people representing what Tchaikovsky created. Without this representation, we wouldn't have had the privilege of experiencing or appreciating the beauty of Tchaikovsky's gift.

So God's answer to the lack of His representation is the great commission, which is the call of God's people to make a personal presentation of the afflictions of Christ to the world. For the present, Christ is not physically on the earth, but we are His body. Therefore, we represent Christ to the unreached people at our schools, work places, our neighborhoods, and our communities. In doing this, we "fill up...what is still lacking in...Christ's afflictions." 2 Corinthians 4:10 says, "We always carry around in our body the death of Jesus, so that the life of Jesus may also be revealed in our body." I heard it once said that the cross of Christ is for propitiation, and our cross is for propagation. Put more plainly: the cross of Christ was for the atonement of our sins; our cross is to spread His atonement to the rest of the world around us.

I can't remember where I read it, but I like this quote from one of my favorite pastor/teachers, Doug Wilson. He said, "Remember that Jesus has a body in this world. You are His hands and feet. But remember also that His hands and feet were pierced."

The suffering and persecution Paul endured *for* the name of Jesus Christ was rarely left out of his preaching *of* Jesus Christ. Persecution and the gospel go hand in hand. Wherever the true gospel is preached, persecution will always follow. And Paul was empowered by his suffering because it brought about many opportunities for his gospel ministry.

In every city the Holy Spirit warns me that *prison and hardships are facing me.* However, I consider my life worth nothing to me; *my only aim is to finish the race and complete the task* the Lord Jesus has given me - *the task of testifying to the good news of God's grace.*
(Acts 20:23-24, emphasis mine)

If we are distressed, it is for your comfort and *salvation.*
(2 Corinthians 1:6, emphasis mine)

And *pray* for us, too, *that God may open a door for our message, so that we may proclaim the mystery of Christ, for which I am in chains.*
(Colossians 4:3, emphasis mine)

We had previously suffered and been treated outrageously in Philippi, as you know, but *with the help of our God we dared to tell you His gospel in the face of strong opposition.*
(1 Thessalonians 2:2, emphasis mine)

And *of this gospel I was appointed* a herald and an
apostle and a teacher. *That is why I am suffering* as I am.
(2 Timothy 1:11-12, emphasis mine)

Remember Jesus Christ, raised from the dead,
descended from David. *This is my gospel, for which
I am suffering...* Therefore *I endure everything for the sake
of the elect, that they too may obtain the salvation*
that is in Christ Jesus, with eternal glory.
(2 Timothy 2:8-10, emphasis mine)

*Everyone who wants to live a godly life
in Christ Jesus will be persecuted.*
(2 Timothy 3:12, emphasis mine)

One would probably assume that persecution and imprisonment
because of one's faith would only decrease the advancement of the
gospel. However, by God's design, Paul was put in prison for the
expansion of it.

Now I want you to know, brothers and sisters, that
*what has happened to me has actually served to advance
the gospel. As a result*, it has become clear throughout
the whole palace guard and to everyone else that
I am in chains for Christ. And *because of my chains*,
most of *the brothers and sisters have become confident
in the Lord and* dare *all the more to proclaim the gospel*
without fear.... *I am put here for the defense of the
gospel.* (Philippians 1:12-14, 16, emphasis mine)

Have you ever read *Foxe's Book of Martyrs*? One thing that
stood out to me while I was reading it was the countless fellow
prisoners, prison guards, and executioners who were converted as
they witnessed the steadfast, unwavering faith of the early church

martyrs as they faced barbaric and merciless torture and death. And I think it would be safe to say any Christian today who is or has been persecuted because of their faith in Christ, would tell us that their suffering has only furthered the advancement of the gospel. By His sovereign hand, when God shuts bars behind His people, He will always open doors for the gospel.

> This is my gospel, for which I am suffering even *to the point of being chained* like a criminal. *But God's word is not chained.*
> (2 Timothy 2:8-9, emphasis mine)

Josef Tson was a Romanian Baptist minister in the 1970's under communist rule. He was arrested and imprisoned several times. Each time he experienced several weeks of severe interrogation, beatings, and mind games before finally being exiled from the country in 1981. His theology on suffering is that tribulation is never an accident, but always a part of God's sovereign plan for building His church. Below is just a portion of his testimony.

> ...I told the interrogator, "spilling my blood would only serve to water the growth of the gospel of Jesus Christ. You should know your supreme weapon is killing. My supreme weapon is dying...Now here is how it works, Sir: You know that my sermons are on tape all over the country. When you shoot me or crush me, whichever way you choose, you only sprinkle my sermons with my blood. Everybody who has a tape of one of my sermons will pick it up and say, 'I had better listen again. This man died for what he preached'. Sir, my sermons will speak 10 times louder after you kill me and because you kill me. In fact, I will conquer this country for God because you killed me. Go on and do it." [5]

Those who have persecuted the Church from its beginnings to present would not have done so if they had any idea what persecution achieves, just like they would not have crucified our Lord if they had known what it would fulfill. Throughout Church history, persecution has only backfired on those who are persecuting, and has only served to further the gospel, producing genuinely devoted and steadfast Christians.

How beautiful are the feet of those who bring the good news!

Romans 10:15

Modern Day Persecution

The task is the same in every generation: If God's Word is to be heard, we who love it must stand in its defense. [6]

~ James R. White

Open Doors USA is a non-profit Christian organization that works to support persecuted Christians around the world. In their 2021 World Watch List (WWL) of the top 50 countries where Christians are most persecuted for their faith, it was reported, from October 2019 to September 2020, that an average of 13 Christians per day were violently killed because of their faith. Below is an excerpt from their report:

> This year, the total number of Christian martyrs increased from 4,305 (WWL 2020) to 4,761 (WWL 2021). Keep in mind that this number is likely to be much lower than the actual reality because, especially in closed countries like North Korea and Afghanistan or conflict-ridden places like Somalia and Libya, killings are often done in secrecy and/

or go unreported. No one in a North Korean prison camp or a Muslim tribe in Somalia is reporting the murder of a Christian. Yet Open Doors has talked to thousands of believers and refugees to know that Christians are dying for their faith—every day.

And David Curry, the president and CEO of Open Doors USA, while introducing the above mentioned report said this:

> The numbers of God's people who are suffering should mean the Church is dying—that Christians are keeping quiet, losing their faith, and turning away from one another...But that's not what's happening. Instead, in living color, we see the words of God recorded in the prophet Isaiah: "I will make a way in the wilderness and rivers in the desert" (Isaiah 43:19, ESV). [7]

I found it interesting that two days after finishing the first draft of this chapter, our pastor, Tom Mertz, started a new series called *This Isn't Safe*. The first sermon of this series was called *Worth Dying For*. God's timing is always impeccable, isn't it? There were a few statements he made that really stuck out to me. With his permission, I felt it was fitting to add them to the end of this chapter. He stated, "In the gospel, we are guaranteed eternal security, but not circumstantial safety. For Christians, there are countries that are more spiritually risky than this one. Bottom line: it's dangerous to follow Jesus, but it's more dangerous not to....The spiritual risks that we have here in America are apathy, complacency, control, materialism, busyness, idolatry, and tribalism."

There will be a day (maybe sooner than some might think) that we, here in America, will begin to lose our freedom of religion. In fact, we have already seen several attacks against our freedoms in the last 15 to 20 years. I think of Jack Phillips as one of many examples in the last decade. His story hits a little closer to home for me, not only because he lives in my home state, but because our families attended the same church together back when I was in high school. Jack is the infamous cake artist who owned Masterpiece Cakeshop in Colorado. In case you don't know his story, he was asked to make a cake for a same-sex couple's wedding, but he politely declined because it would go against his faith. Because of his stand for truth, he has had to endure targeted attacks against him and his business for over 8 years to live accordingly with his faith. However, even after winning his initial case in the Supreme Court, he continues to be attacked and set up for more allegations which continue to drag him back to court. Nevertheless, Jack has been willing to stand in the face of this persecution, even knowing the cost he would pay and the possibility of losing everything. He has been an inspiration to me personally, as well as countless others.

We must not think it strange when we are oppressed and persecuted for our faith (1 Peter 4:12; 1 Thessalonians 3:3). It is the price we choose to pay when we choose to follow Jesus. He paid His life for ours; in turn we should be willing to lose everything for Him.

Conclusion

First, we were saved by the gospel. Second, we are being sanctified by way of the gospel. Last, but *not* least, we are to share the gospel with others who need to hear it. This was God's plan from the beginning. Not because He needs us, but because He wants to use us. He strategically puts us where we need to be in order to effectively spread the good news of His kingdom to those around us.

Paul left us examples of how we are to spread the gospel; through our words *and* our suffering. Paul exhibits the sufferings of Christ by suffering himself for those he is trying to win to Christ. In his sufferings they see Christ's sufferings. The gospel never has advanced without it. Our best witness is in our worst circumstances.

I have to admit, while writing this chapter I have been convicted of my own lethargic faith in the face of sharing the gospel. I only pray that God would give us the resolve and fortitude needed to boldly proclaim the gospel, enduring any persecution that might come (menial as it may be) rejoicing as the early church did because they were counted worthy of suffering for His Name. The only way we can do this is to continually remind ourselves that, just as our own faith is a gift, our suffering for Christ and His gospel is a gift as well (Philippians 1:29).

+++++++

Therefore, among God's churches we boast about your perseverance and faith in all the persecutions and trials you are enduring.

2 THESSALONIANS 1:4

The Gift of Glorifying God

*The best possible end of all of God's actions is ultimately His glory.
That is, all that God does or allows in all of His
creation will ultimately serve His glory.* [1]

~ *Jerry Bridges*

This chapter is our 6th and final *why:* The Gift of Suffering for God's Glory. So far we've seen how God commissions and purposes our pain pertaining to ourselves, and then pertaining to others. Now we are going to focus all of our attention on God; for God and His glory far surpass the previous 5 *whys*. For it is His glory that is the culmination and chief end of *everything*.

Have you ever thought about suffering for the fame and splendor of someone else? As an Olympic athlete would, we can understand *willingly* putting our own bodies through pain and stress to accomplish an end goal resulting in our *own* fame and glory. But suffering so that someone else would obtain the praise rather than us is hard to reckon with; especially when it's God. We know that He deserves all praise and honor and glory, but how does God use our suffering to accomplish His own renown? Better yet, why does God need to use our suffering to bring Himself glory, especially when He's already receiving it from the whole earth (Psalm 66:4; Romans 11:36)?

By the end of this chapter I hope to have answered these two questions. However, before we start, I want to lay down some ground work. I want us to put aside our underlying assumptions that God would never ask us to suffer *just* so He can look good. He does! And above all things, we must submit to the power, splendor, and majesty of the King of the universe. If we can't bow our knee to this idea of suffering for His glory — the only proper posture before this awesome King — we will never fully be able to grasp any understanding of His true character as it relates to our pain and His glory. I'd like you to read this quote from John Piper a couple times before you continue on in this chapter.

> My feelings are not God. God is God. My feelings
> do not define truth. God's word defines truth.
> My feelings are echoes and responses to what my
> mind perceives. And sometimes - many times -
> my feelings are out of sync with the truth. When
> that happens - and it happens every day in some
> measure - I try not to bend the truth to justify my
> imperfect feelings, but rather, I plead with God:
> Purify my perceptions of your truth and transform
> my feelings so that they are in sync with the truth. [2]

God is All About His Glory

Scripture says that all glory belongs to God (John 17:5; Acts 7:55), that God will not share His glory with any other (Isaiah 42:8), that God reveals His glory (Colossians 1:27; Psalm 72:19; Isaiah 6:3), and that God created us for His glory (Isaiah 43:7; Romans 9:23). The noun, glory, is found 606 times in our English Bibles. 376 in the

Old Testament, and 230 in the New Testament. God is *all* about His own glory!

The Westminster Shorter Catechism is a document all orthodox Christians have recognized as stating the essentials of our faith since 1648. In its very first tenet (a Biblical doctrine shown in a question and answer form) says: (Q.)"What is the chief end of man?" (A.)"Man's chief end is to glorify God and enjoy Him forever." In simpler terms, the real question is this: Why do we exist? And the answer is: To bring glory to God. This is everyone's ultimate purpose, no matter what we are doing or what is happening to us. We think so small; so selfishly. We think there is a purpose unto ourselves and all we want is to understand it. But it's so much bigger than us, and we must look to the higher purpose which is outside of ourselves — God's glory.

Just for fun, here is a little word study to help us jump start our understanding of the meaning behind God's glory. Our English word *glory* comes from the Latin *gloria* which means fame or renown. From Old French, *glorie* means worldly honor, renown, splendor, to glory in, or boast. The Greek word, *doxa*, means brightness, splendor, radiance, or magnificence. The Hebrew word which is used for glory in the Old Testament means heaviness or weightiness. And finally, the verb *to glorify* means to ascribe honor and praise.

God's name is distinguished. It is linked with the word glory. They cannot be separated. His reputation, throughout all the universe, is derived from His magnificence and His splendor. As believers, we should always strive to bring God honor. Everything we do should glorify Him. Paul tells the Church of Corinth that no matter what they do, even eating and drinking, should be done with the intention of glorifying God (1 Corinthians 10:31). We should strive to honor Him in our actions because we are His representatives to the world, and when we fail to honor Him in our actions we are sinning against Him. Here's another quote by John Piper taken from a sermon he preached at the Plenary Session — a conference for pastors in 2015:

What is sin? It is the glory of God not honored. The holiness of God not reverenced. The greatness of God not admired. The power of God not praised. The truth of God not sought. The wisdom of God not esteemed. The beauty of God not treasured. The goodness of God not savored. The faithfulness of God not trusted. The commandments of God not obeyed. The justice of God not respected. The wrath of God not feared. The grace of God not cherished. The presence of God not prized. The person of God not loved. That is sin. [3]

God, for some reason that I may never understand, chose to create us in His own image (Genesis 1:27), *and* for His own glory.

Bring my sons from afar and my daughters from the ends of the earth — everyone who is called by my name, *whom I created for my glory*, whom I formed and made. (Isaiah 43: 6-7, emphasis mine)

The wild animals honor me...because I provide water in the wilderness...[I] give drink to my people, my chosen, *the people I formed for myself that they may proclaim my praise*. (Isaiah 43:20-21, emphasis mine)

For from Him [Jesus] and through Him and *for Him are all things. To Him be the glory forever!* Amen. (Romans 11:36, emphasis mine)

God created us for His good pleasure. All of creation was intended to give Him honor. *Everything* He does, as the sovereign King of the Universe, is for His own glory — and He knows He is worthy of it. It is neither selfish of Him to want it, nor does He hide the fact that He deserves it. Scripture says that He is jealous for

His Holy name (Ezekiel 39:25). Unlike us, God is wholly Holy and without sin, therefore He has no pride that could set Himself up to demand undeserved attention and glory. I love how God speaks about Himself in Isaiah 42:8. He says, "I am the LORD; *that is My name! I will not give My glory* to another, Nor My praise to graven images" (NASB, emphasis mine).

So instead of unjustly judging His motives, crafting a God of our own imagination and desires — which is prideful — let's look at the God who is actually in the text. Let us properly acknowledge God and praise Him appropriately as David did.

> *The heavens declare the glory of God;*
> *   the skies proclaim the work of His hands.*
> *Day after day they pour forth speech;*
> *   night after night they reveal knowledge.*
> *They have no speech, they use no words;*
> *   no sound is heard from them.*
> *Yet their voice goes out into all the earth,*
> *   their words to the ends of the world.*
> *In the heavens God has pitched a tent for the sun.*
> *   It is like a bridegroom coming out of his chamber,*
> *   like a champion rejoicing to run his course.*
> *It rises at one end of the heavens*
> *   and makes its circuit to the other;*
> *   nothing is deprived of its warmth.*
> *The law of the Lord is perfect,*
> *   refreshing the soul.*
> *The statues of the Lord are trustworthy,*
> *   making wise the simple.*
> *The precepts of the Lord are right,*
> *   giving joy to the heart.*
> *The commands of the Lord are radiant,*
> *   giving light to the eyes.*
> *The fear of the Lord is pure,*

enduring forever.
The decrees of the Lord are firm,
and all of them are righteous.
They are more precious than gold,
than much pure gold;
they are sweeter than honey,
than honey from the honeycomb.
By them your servant is warned;
in keeping them there is great reward.
But who can discern their own errors?
Forgive my hidden faults.
Keep your servant also from willful sins;
may they not rule over me.
Then I will be blameless,
innocent of great transgression.
May these words of my mouth
and this meditation of my heart
be pleasing in your sight,
LORD, my Rock and my Redeemer.

PSALM 19

For the Sake and Honor of His Name

A person with a reputable character provides someone with a good name. Does someone in particular come to mind who is known for their reputation? Whether good or bad? A family member, a friend, a leader in the community, an employer, fellow employees, a pastor, a professional entertainer. How about you? Are you concerned about your reputation? *Your* good name?

I would bet most of us actually do care about what other people think of us. Now, I'm not talking about vanity here, but character. Of course we want a good name. When other people hear our names, we want them to have a positive image come to their minds, as we should, since we want to live with godly character. We are God's representatives, after all. King Solomon says, "A good name is more desirable than great riches; to be esteemed is better than silver or gold" (Proverbs 22:1). Our influence, whether good or bad, can go far more widespread than we could ever think it will, and sometimes it can go beyond our grave.

My Opa (grandfather) was a man of integrity. His upstanding reputation was well known in his community, and he was loved by all who knew him. He was highly esteemed by his family and within his church. All I had to do was mention that I was his granddaughter, and people would automatically give me the same admiration and respect. I was connected to him, therefore benefitting from his reputation. However, on the flip side, my own personal behavior could inevitably affect his reputation. Hypothetically, let's say I was known for my delinquency and running with the wrong crowd. This behavior would embarrass him and disgrace him in the public eye.

In the Old Testament, God chose the nation of Israel to be His representation to the rest of the world. Israel's conformity to God's law was intended to make a distinction between them and the pagan nations surrounding them. God wanted to show His glory and power through them, so all nations would know and fear the one true, living God (1 Kings 8:41-43). Instead, as a whole, the nation of Israel was characterized by covenant rebellion. Their corrupt and immoral behavior profaned God's name and dishonored His character. However, because God had made a covenant with Abraham, promising to bless his seed and to make his offspring as numerous as the stars in the sky, He remained faithful to His word, even though God knew that His people would be unfaithful. This is why the covenant He made with Abraham was one-sided (Genesis 15:9-21). The author of Hebrews said that "there was no one greater for Him to swear by, [so] He swore by Himself" (Hebrews 6:13-15), meaning that He swore on His own Name to keep His promise to Abraham and his descendants.

And, as expected, Israel dishonored and profaned His name. After 800-plus years of disobeying God's law, He scattered them among the nations.

> *I dispersed them among the nations*, and they were scattered through the countries; *I judged them according to their conduct and their actions*. And wherever they went among the nations they profaned my holy name, for it was said of them, "These are the LORD's people, and yet they had to leave His land." *I had a concern for my holy name, which the people of Israel profaned among the nations where they had gone*. (Ezekiel 36:19-21, emphasis mine)

Keeping His Promises for His Name's Sake

Regardless of Israel's sinful disobedience, God kept His promise according to His covenants with Abraham, Moses, and David, and restored the kingdom of Israel. However, it was not for any virtue on Israel's part, but rather in spite of their corrupt behavior, and all for His name's sake. It brings Him glory and honor when He is faithful in keeping His promises, *especially* to those who have been unfaithful.

> I will accept you as fragrant incense when I bring you out from the nations and gather you from the countries where you have been scattered, and *I will be proved holy through you in the sight of the nations*. Then you will know that I am the LORD, when I bring you into the land of Israel, *the land I had sworn with uplifted hand to give to your ancestors*. There you will remember your conduct and all the actions by which you have defiled yourselves, and you will

loathe yourselves for all the evil you have done. *You will know that I am the LORD, when I deal with you for my name's sake and not according to your evil ways and your corrupt practices*, you people of Israel, declares the Sovereign LORD. (Ezekiel 20:41-44, emphasis mine)

Therefore say to the Israelites, "This is what the Sovereign LORD says: *It is not for your sake*, people of Israel, that I am going to do these things, *but for the sake of my holy name*, which you have profaned among the nations where you have gone. *I will show the holiness of my great name*...Then the nations will know that I am the LORD, declares the Sovereign LORD, when I am *proved holy through you* before their eyes. For I will take you out of the nations; I will gather you from all the countries and bring you back into your own land." (Ezekiel 36:22-24, emphasis mine)

Daniel was among the men King Nebuchadnezzar carried off into exile. After arriving in Babylon, he was hand-picked, along with several others, to serve in the king's palace. After just a short time, Daniel ended up being made ruler over the entire province of Babylon and was placed in charge over all the king's wise men.

He knew the prophecies Jeremiah spoke concerning the exile to Babylon, including the prophecy that their captivity would only last for 70 years (Jeremiah 25:1-14, 29:10-14; 2 Chronicles 36:21). Recognizing where he was in the prophetic timeline, Daniel went to his knees, pleading with the Lord to have mercy upon "the city that bears [His] name", and to forgive their sin. Daniel understood that God's great name was at stake in keeping with His promise to bring them back to their land. At the end of Daniel's prayer he cries out:

Now, our God, hear the prayers and petitions of
your servant. *For your sake, Lord,* look with favor
on your desolate sanctuary. Give ear, our God, and
hear; *open your eyes and see the desolation of the city
that bears your Name.* We do not make requests of
you because we are righteous, but because of your
great mercy. *Lord, listen! Lord, forgive! Lord, hear and
act! For your sake, my God, do not delay, because your
city and your people bear your Name.* (Daniel 9:17-19,
emphasis mine)

Daniel almost sounds demanding, doesn't he? He was very
direct and adamant for God to act according to His promise. It's
because Daniel knew God's character which gave him confidence
that God would keep His promises. He knew that when God
delivered His people, His name would be honored. And we can
see from his prayer that this was his greatest desire too – for God's
name to again be glorified. And, soon after, God acted on His
promise and sent a remnant back to Jerusalem to rebuild the temple
(Ezra 1:1-6) — *for the sake of His great Name.*

Our Salvation and forgiveness for His Name's Sake

Just as we've learned above that God is most glorified when He
is faithful to keep His promises, we also see that He is also most
glorified when He extends His mercy and forgiveness to undeserving
people. The prayer that we just read above from Daniel has been
my example over the years to ensure I'm in the right posture when
I am petitioning God on such matters as salvation and forgiveness.
When praying for the salvation of lost family members or friends,
our number one desire should be that God would extend His mercy,
not only for their sake, but more so for the sake of *His* great name.
If our prayers for the lost were to model Daniel's, I believe they
would sound something like the following:

Lord of heaven, you are the God that heals. Not just the healing of bodies, but the healing of souls. You are the only one who can open eyes to see you and open ears to hear you. Therefore, I plead with you, on behalf of _____, according to your will, have mercy on their soul, for your name's sake. Do not only save for their sake, but for yours. Show your mercy so they, and those around them, will praise and glorify your name, proclaiming your mercy and grace, and declaring that you only are the God who can save.

> Yet He saved them *for His name's sake,*
> *to make His mighty power known.*
> (Psalms 106:8, emphasis mine)

I, even I, am He who blots out your transgressions, *for my own sake*, and remembers your sins no more.
(Isaiah 43:25, emphasis mine)

Therefore the LORD waits to be gracious unto you, and therefore *He exalts Himself to show mercy on you.*
(Isaiah 30:18, ESV, emphasis mine)

And when it comes to asking God for forgiveness, our request should be rooted in the same desire to bring glory to His name. Because when we confess our sin and ask for forgiveness, we are proclaiming Jesus Christ's death, burial, and resurrection. Anytime His mercy and grace is magnified, His glory and renown is made known. Similarly, may our prayer for forgiveness sound something like this:

> Forgive me, Lord, according to your promises (Micah 7:18-19) and for the greatness of your

Name's sake. Not for me, but for your grace which is glorified through the forgiveness found in Jesus Christ. Oh God, who are you that you should forgive such a sinner like me? And yet, you have promised to blot out my sin (Isaiah 43:25). I can do nothing but praise you for your mercy.

For the sake of your name, LORD,
forgive my iniquity, though it is great.
(Psalm 25:11, emphasis mine)

Although our sins testify against us, *do something,
LORD, for the sake of your name*. For we have often
rebelled; we have sinned against you.
(Jeremiah 14:7, emphasis mine)

I am writing to you, little children, because
your sins have been forgiven you for His name's sake.
(1 John 2:12, NASB, emphasis mine)

Being Concerned With His Glory Results In Our Good

*Nearly everyone used mightily by God in scripture suffered. If
we read some of the prayers of the sufferers, we noticed that,
for the most part, they were concerned not primarily
with their own comfort but with the glory of God.* [4]

~ Chris Tiegreen

As already stated, all of creation is for God and His glory (Romans 11:36). The amazing thing for us is: when we are concerned for His glory, all that exalts God is also working for our ultimate good. Everything He does for His sake results in the benefit of our salvation and for our eternal enjoyment in Him. Therefore, every promised trial and difficult circumstance which refines us, every time we are disciplined bringing restoration, and every time we have the opportunity to comfort others and share the gospel through our suffering, ultimately glorifies God because we are calling on His name, trusting in His promises, and pointing others to Christ.

> See, I have refined you, though not as silver;
> I have tested you in the furnace of affliction.
> *For my own sake, for my own sake, I do this.*
> *How can I let myself be defamed?*
> I will not yield my glory to another.
> (Isaiah 48:10-11, emphasis mine)

God repeats Himself in the verse above for emphasis. He assures us that our testing is for Him. He sacrifices our comfort for the higher purpose of making His own glory known. I heard it once said, He uses our story for His glory. And Louie Giglio, in his video series, *Grace [The One And Only]*, says that we are trophies of God's grace. Therefore, our scars that result from our suffering and sanctification become the stories of God's victories.

> *This is to my Father's glory*, that you bear much
> fruit, showing yourselves to be my disciples.
> (John 15:8, emphasis mine)

> As [Jesus] went along, He saw a man blind from birth.
> His disciples asked Him, "Rabbi, who sinned,
> this man or his parents, that he was born blind?"
> "Neither this man nor his parents sinned," said Jesus, "but
> *this happened so that the works of God [His glory]*
> *might be displayed in him."*
> (John 9:1–3, emphasis mine)

Though now for a little while you may have
had to suffer grief in all kinds of trials.
*These have come so that the proven genuineness
of your faith* - of greater worth than gold, which
parishes even though refined by fire – *may result in praise,
glory and honor* when Jesus Christ is revealed.
(1 Peter 1:6-7, emphasis mine)

But *you are a chosen people*, a royal priesthood,
a holy nation, God's special possession, *that you may
declare the praises of Him who called you* out of
darkness into His wonderful light.
(1 Peter 2:9, emphasis mine)

In Him we were also chosen, having been predestined
*according to the plan of Him who works out everything in
conformity with the purpose of His will, in order that we,*
who were the first to put our hope in Christ,
might be for the praise of His glory.
(Ephesians 1:11-12, emphasis mine)

But *He said to me,* "My grace is sufficient for you, for *my power
is made perfect in weakness."* Therefore I will boast all the
more gladly about my weaknesses, *so that Christ's power may
rest on me.* That is why, for Christ's sake, I delight in weaknesses,
in insults, and hardships, in persecutions, in difficulties.
For when I am weak, then I am strong.
(2 Corinthians 12:9–10, emphasis mine)

In the verse above, Paul points out that Christ's all-sufficient grace is magnified through our weakness, or rather, our suffering. When we rely on Him in our distress, His strength becomes our strength, and we show the world that He is more desirable than anything we have lost. This is why Paul boasts in his weakness: so that Christ's power may be evident in him while he is suffering. Our suffering is not only designed to remove us from self-reliance to grace-dependence, but to magnify Christ through it all. Our trials are an amplifier to what is in our hearts, and if Jesus lives in us, then our highest value in life should be to glorify God.

This next verse is one of my favorites.

> For *God,* who *said, "Let light shine out of darkness,"*
> made His light shine in our hearts to *give us the light*
> *of the knowledge of God's glory displayed in the face*
> *of Christ.* But we have this treasure in jars of clay
> *to show that this all-surpassing power is from God*
> *and not from us.* We are hard pressed on every side,
> but not crushed; perplexed, but not in despair; persecuted,
> but not abandoned; struck down, but not destroyed.
> (2 Corinthians 4:6-9, emphasis mine)

There are many places in scripture that refer to God as a potter and to us as lumps of clay (Isaiah 64:8; Jeremiah 18:1-4; Job 10:9; Romans 9:21). The verse above is just another example of likening us to jars of clay. Its focus, however, is on the light of the gospel which has been put into our hearts - our hearts being likened to jars of clay. As you well know, jars of clay are relatively weak and can break pretty easily when put under a lot of pressure or dropped. Paul is saying that the gospel of Christ – this light that shines out of the darkness – has been contained within our hearts. Moreover, this "all-surpassing power" that he mentions is the same power that raised Jesus from the dead. It is *this* power that has been put into our jars of clay.

It's an understatement to say that on their own, jars of clay would *never* be able to hold this kind of power without being crushed and destroyed. Ironically though, those of us who have put our faith in Christ's finished work, and whom God "made His light shine in our hearts," are actually strengthened and upheld by it. Without this power in us, when hard times come, we would be crushed, perplexed, abandoned, and destroyed. But because we do have this light, this "all-surpassing power" shining within our hearts of clay, we are not crushed when hard pressed. We do not fall into despair when we are perplexed. We are not abandoned when we are persecuted. And we are not destroyed when we are struck down. This is *all* to show the power and glory of Him who holds us together.

The total sum of our lives exists to display the glory of God. It is only when we surrender to our Potter, acknowledging that we are only clay in His hands, that we will find our sole purpose and truest joy in Him. Andrew Murray captures this thought with one of my favorite quotes:

> The highest glory of the creature is in being only a vessel, to receive and enjoy and show forth the glory of God. It can do this only as it is willing to be nothing in itself, that God may be all. [5]

Conclusion

God is concerned for His Name (Ezekiel 36: 21). All that He does is for the sake of upholding the integrity, reputation, and holiness of His Name, and He doesn't hide the fact that He knows He is worthy of it all (Ezekiel 39:25). The interest in His own glory is the basis for all of His actions. We see this when we read passages that say, "for my Name's sake," and "not for our sake," but "for Your sake."

Nonetheless, God's glory and our good are not at odds with each other. He is most magnified to keep His promises and to save His people. God purposes our pain for our benefit, but the chief end is for His glory. And it is His glory that should be our most valued treasure, using the platform of our suffering to display it.

Therefore, we should always aim to bring glory to God in and through our circumstances — be it in good times or bad.

———————— ·✦✦✦✦· ————————

We pray this so that the name of our Lord Jesus may be glorified in you, and you in Him, according to the grace of our God and the Lord Jesus Christ.

2 THESSALONIANS 1:12

8

The User Guide: Attitudes In Our Suffering

Be joyful in hope, patient in affliction, faithful in prayer.

ROMANS 12:12

I have just presented us with 6 biblical reasons why we suffer, but more importantly, why each of these reasons are gifts. Here's a quick recap:

1. We suffer because God has *promised us this gift of suffering when following Jesus.*
2. We suffer so that we can be given the *gift of sanctification,* which is the refining process that fashions us into the image of His Son, allowing us to share in His eternal glory.
3. We suffer for the *gift of discipline* from a loving and kind Father who wants an intimate relationship with His children.
4. We suffer so we can be given the *gift of comfort,* allowing us to minister God's comfort to others.

5. We suffer so we can spread the *gift of the Gospel*, playing a crucial part in the expansion of His kingdom.
6. We suffer so we may have the *gift of glorifying God* – the Giver of all good gifts.

As you've been reading through these pages, I hope you've been imagining God assembling and packaging this gift of our suffering, starting with the box of His sovereignty and then placing each of these six gifts inside. Now if you think about it, most gifts that come in a box include a user manual or an instruction guide of some kind. I want us to read this chapter as if it is the user guide that comes with our gift — the instructions on how to successfully maintain the right attitude while God is sovereignly applying this gift to our lives.

Attitude Check

I'm going to let you in on a little secret. I'm really writing this chapter for me. Of course, I want you to benefit from this too, but truth be told, I kind of stink at this part. I often give the appearance that I have my attitude in check, however, I know my heart better than anyone, and God knows it even better than I do. I would hate to see my *attitude report card* from God because I know it would be worse than I can imagine.

Have you ever been told that you needed an attitude check? I heard it often as I was growing into the typical know-it-all teenager. I don't know about you, but it really annoyed me. The first time I heard it used I thought, "What is this new lingo coming out of my parents' mouths? What does that even mean, and why would I even need one?" However, even though these words were new to me back then, the concept behind their meaning has been around for millennia. Even David understood what an "attitude check" meant. He prayed, "Search me, God, and know my heart; *test me and know my anxious thoughts.* See if there is any offensive way in me, and lead me in the way everlasting." (Psalm 139:23-24, emphasis mine).

(See also Psalm 26:2-3). David didn't want anything hindering his relationship with God, even bad attitudes.

We all know it's not easy to examine our attitudes (let alone admit we need to). Often we just want to succumb to the despair we are feeling at any given time. It's more than obvious when my husband or I are feeling this way. When we ask each other what is wrong, the answer is often: "Life!" However, as soon as I hear that single-word answer come out of our mouths, it immediately registers in my spirit that we need an attitude check.

Actually, I just had one of these moments this morning. Today marks the 26th birthday of our first son, Tyler, who I delivered stillborn. It hit me harder than I thought it would this year (probably because my whole focus recently has been on writing this book). Anyway, Phil asked me what was wrong, and what was my answer? "Life!" Ugh! My attitude check alarm went off. And what better timing — just before sitting down to write *this* chapter.

Attitude of Complaining

After all the miraculous things God performed for the Israelites as He brought them out of Egypt, all they could do was complain. Instead of acknowledging God's provision and goodness toward them, they threw it back in His face and told Moses that they were better off in Egypt (Exodus 14:12). This attitude that God's people began to acquire displeased Him considerably. Numbers 11:1 says, "Now the people complained about their hardships in the hearing of the LORD, and when He heard them His anger was aroused. Then fire from the LORD burned among them and consumed some of the outskirts of the camp."

We don't want to be like the Israelites, only focusing on our hardships in the wilderness rather than fixing our eyes on all the good things that God has done for us. They stopped trusting in

Him and forgot His promise to guide them, provide for them, and to deliver them from their enemies. In doing so, all they did was contribute to their own suffering. When we turn our eyes away from God, forget His promises, and stop acknowledging God's provision and goodness in our lives, we're essentially doing the same thing. We become contributors to our own pain. The only way to gain traction from sliding down this slope is to keep our attitudes in check by using God's Word. And remember, when we don't keep our attitudes in check, we are dishonoring God.

For the word of God is alive and active. Sharper than any double-edged sword, it penetrates even to dividing soul and spirit, joints and marrow; it *judges the thoughts and attitudes of the heart.* (Hebrews 4:12, emphasis mine).

Nothing in all of creation is hidden from God's sight. The Word of God judges our thoughts and attitudes! "Everything is uncovered and laid bare before the eyes of Him to whom we must give account" (Hebrews 4:13) — even our attitudes. However, His Word also is given to us for our encouragement, our endurance, and our hope (Romans 15:4).

There are several key points we need to look at in our user guide to help us get the most joy out of this gift of suffering. It is a circular pattern that we need to continually work through. Suffering produces hope for our future glory, and our future hope then produces joy. Joy in our future hope produces right attitudes and proper perspectives, which then fuel our anticipation for this hope. This in turn gives us the focus, fortitude, and faithfulness needed as we come back to the beginning of our suffering. And as you can see, everything is centered around our hope.

I pray that the scripture shared in this chapter will penetrate our hearts and minds, encouraging us to have joy, humility, patience, focus, fortitude, and faithfulness while we suffer, in turn giving us the right perspective with an attitude of anticipation for our hope of glory.

> *Without this heart attitude it is exceedingly difficult*
> *for us to accept the circumcision of the flesh.* [1]
>
> ~ *Watchman Nee*

Joy in Our Hope

As Christians, we live in a paradoxical world. The Bible tells us that when we are weak, we are strong (2 Corinthians 12:10). When we were poor, we became rich (2 Corinthians 8:9). We have been freed to become slaves (Romans 6:22). We died so we can live (2 Corinthians 5:15; Colossians 3:3). We are blessed in our persecution (Matthew 5:10-11) and have joy in our suffering (James 1:2). These are paradoxes that cannot live outside of Christ. They are only possible because of the cross. Therefore, our joy can only live if it is centered in Christ and His promises.

The joy in a believer's life should look much different from that of an unbeliever. For the unbeliever, joy (happiness) is contingent on their happenings. It's a surface-level emotion based on external factors. On the other hand, as believers, our joy is not dependent on our circumstances. Our joy is deeply rooted in a firm foundation — Jesus Christ. Happiness is momentary, but true joy in Jesus is eternal.

God wants us to find our ultimate and most satisfying joy in Him. Nehemiah is a great example of this as he encouraged the returning exiled Israelites to find their joy in God. This joy was where they would find the source of their strength when they were feeling defeated (Nehemiah 8:10). Likewise, our source of strength can also be found in the joy we have in Jesus. We can do this by fixing our minds on Jesus and the hope of our reward, which He secured through His death and resurrection (Hebrews 12:2). When we rejoice in this promise of eternity with Him, it deepens our hope and makes bearing our trials seem small in comparison. It gives us the strength to keep pressing forward. Paul gives us a good example of this when he states:

We rejoice in our sufferings, knowing that
suffering produces endurance,
and endurance produces character,
and *character produces hope.*
(Romans 5:3–4, ESV, emphasis mine).

As Paul explains, our suffering solidifies our hope and our joy is sustained by our hope. Paul was stripped of everything, yet because Christ was his focus, he could find joy through all his circumstances (Philippians 4:12; 1 Thessalonians 5:16-18). There was no imprisonment or threat of death that could shake his faith or dismantle his joy. Everything boiled down to his future hope found in Christ. I heard it once said that joy is grace (past, present, and future) recognized.

Like Paul, James encouraged his readers to consider their trials pure joy (James 1:2). Following their own advice, the apostles rejoiced that they could suffer for His name (Acts 5:41). Peter adds that our trials also develop "inexpressible and glorious joy" because we are "receiving the end result of [our] faith, the salvation of [our] souls" (1 Peter 1:7-9). We cannot have the right attitude about our circumstances unless we have joy that is grounded in our hope of eternal glory.

Consider it pure joy, my brothers and sisters,
whenever you face trials of many kinds, because you know
that the testing of your faith produces perseverance.
(James 1:2, emphasis mine)

The apostles left the Sanhedrin, *rejoicing* because they had
been *counted worthy of suffering* disgrace for the Name.
(Acts 5:41, emphasis mine)

In all this you greatly rejoice, though now *for a little while you may*
have had to *suffer grief* in all kinds of trials. *These have come so that*

the proven genuineness of your faith…may result in praise, glory and
honor when Jesus is revealed….[Because] you believe in Him [you] *are
filled with an inexpressible and glorious joy, for you are receiving
the end result of your faith*, the salvation of your souls.
(1 Peter 1:6-9, emphasis mine)

But rejoice inasmuch *as you participate in the sufferings* of
Christ, *so that you may be overjoyed when His glory is revealed.*
(1 Peter 4:13, emphasis mine)

I am greatly encouraged; in all our troubles
my joy knows no bounds.
(2 Corinthians 7:4, emphasis mine)

For Christ sake, *I delight in* weakness, in insults, in hardships,
in persecutions, in difficulties. For when I am weak, then I am strong.
(2 Corinthians 12:10, emphasis mine)

Though the fig tree does not bud and there are no grapes on
the vines, though the olive crop fails and the fields produce no food,
though there are no sheep in the pen and no cattle in the stalls,
Yet I will rejoice in the LORD, I will be joyful in God my Savior.
(Habakkuk 3:17-18, emphasis mine)

Our praise stems from joy. The more difficult our trials are,
the louder our praise should be. Charles Spurgeon considered our
praise to God in times of trouble as the "baseline" of our life's song.
I know this from personal experience. When I sing His praises
through my suffering, my joy is elevated. David invites the afflicted
to rejoice with him (Psalm 34:1-3). The psalmist who wrote Psalm
66, starting with praise and worship, transitions to acknowledging
the trials and suffering that God gave, all while continuing to praise
Him for His faithfulness and love.

Keeping the Perspective of Our Hope

The person who forgets the ultimate is a slave to the immediate.
Don't take your eyes off of the big picture.

~ Unknown

In his first letter, Peter reminds his readers that their trials are temporary and their future hope is eternal. If we could truly grasp the weight of glory that overshadows our temporary pain, I believe our faith would never waiver. As Timothy Keller once said, "If we knew what God knows, we would ask exactly for what He gives."

Even the greatest amount of suffering will seem trivial when we look back on it from heaven. We may now be overwhelmed and heartbroken, but we are only living in the interim. Our life here is short-term. Our joy banks on the perspective that God, in His sovereignty, has ordained each and every trial and has caused every ounce of our pain to shape us into the image of His Son. This is why we can confidently say with the Saints:

Weeping may stay for the night,
but rejoicing comes in the morning.
(Psalm 30:5, emphasis mine)

And the God of all grace, who called you to His eternal glory
in Christ, *after you have suffered a little while, will Himself
restore you and make you strong, firm and steadfast.*
(1 Peter 5:10, emphasis mine)

For our *light and momentary troubles* are achieving for us an
eternal glory that far outweighs them all. *So we fix our eyes*
not on what is seen, but *on what is unseen*, since what
is seen is temporary, but *what is unseen is eternal.*
(2 Corinthians 4:17–18, emphasis mine)

I consider that our present *sufferings are not worth comparing with the glory* that will be revealed in us.
(Romans 8:18, emphasis mine)

Yes, I will continue to rejoice, for I know that through your prayers and God's provision of the Spirit of Jesus Christ *what has happened to me will turn out for my deliverance.*
(Philippians 1:18-19, emphasis mine)

But we have this treasure in jars of clay to show that this all-surpassing power is from God and not from us. *We are hard pressed on every side, but not crushed; perplexed, but not in despair; persecuted, but not abandoned; struck down, but not destroyed.*
(2 Corinthians 4:7-9, emphasis mine)

As servants of God we commend ourselves in every way: in great endurance; in troubles, hardships and distresses; in beatings, imprisonments and riots; in hard work, sleepless nights and hunger; in purity, understanding, patience and kindness; in the Holy Spirit and in sincere love; in truthful speech and in the power of God; with weapons of righteousness in the right hand and in the left; through glory and dishonor, bad report and good report; genuine, yet regarded as impostors; known, yet regarded as unknown; dying, and *yet we live on;* beaten, and *yet not killed;* sorrowful, *yet always rejoicing;* poor, *yet making many rich;* having nothing, and *yet possessing everything.*
(2 Corinthians 6:4-10, emphasis mine)

But He said to me, "My grace is sufficient for you, for my power is made perfect in weakness." Therefore *I will boast all the more gladly about my weaknesses,* so that Christ's power may rest on me.
(2 Corinthians 12:9, emphasis mine)

The Anticipation of Our Hope

You've probably heard the phrase "Life is a journey, not a destination." Well, yes and no. As Christians, we are definitely on a journey through this life. The Bible refers to us as sojourners (1 Peter 2:11). This is a term that can refer to a person who is just passing through, as on a journey. However, we are not just here to travel through this life, but we are on this journey for the destination.

What is it that's capturing your anticipation on this journey? I hope it's not the next new job, car, or house. Our anticipation shouldn't be on anything material. It should be on the eternal. I wonder how much more wisely we would spend our time and money if we focused on the eternal . We are not of this world. We are merely passing through, and our destination is far greater than we can imagine.

They are not of the world, even as I [Jesus] am not of it.
(John 17:16, emphasis mine)

Rejoice and be glad, because *great is your reward in heaven*.
(Matthew 5:12, emphasis added)

As a result *you will be counted worthy of the
kingdom of God, for which you were suffering*.
(2 Thessalonians 1:5, emphasis added)

Be patient and *stand firm*, because *the Lord's coming is near*.
(James 5:8, emphasis added)

Focusing On Our Hope

The focus on our eternal future should override any uncertainty about our present *temporal* life. It's not always easy though. There are times when my chronic pain causes my emotional and mental strength to wane, making me unsure of what the future will be like even in just a few short years. Yet, when I begin to feel overwhelmed in this way, the only thing that helps me withstand the fear is to refocus my eyes on my promised inheritance (1 Peter 1:4).

Philippians 4:1 says: "Therefore, my brothers and sisters... stand firm in the Lord in this way, dear friends!" After Paul tells them to stand firm he tells them how to do it by saying "in this way". But in what way was Paul telling his readers to stand firm? For context we need to read the verses around it. Paul gives us the answer in the prior 2 verses of the previous chapter (Philippians 3:20-21). Remember, when Paul was writing his letters, there were no chapters and verses. So the combined 3 verses that we have in our Bible's between chapters 3 and 4 was one continuous thought. Without the chapters and verses it reads like this:

> But our citizenship is in heaven. And *we eagerly await a Savior from there*, the Lord Jesus Christ, *who*, by the power that enables Him to bring everything under His control, *will transform our lowly bodies so that they will be like His glorious body. Therefore, my brothers and sisters*, you whom I love and long for, my joy and crown, *stand firm in the Lord in this way*, dear friend!

The word *therefore* is a conjunctive adverb, which indicates the relationship between two independent clauses. One of my favorite sayings I've heard from several theologians is, "We have to ask why this *therefore* is there for?" Simply put, Paul is telling his readers that we stand firm, *therefore*, by eagerly awaiting — putting our focusing on — our Savior, knowing that when the time comes He will transform our bodies to be like His.

When we die, the hope of our once-future glory will finally be realized. We will awake from this life to the next and see the face of whom we have been conformed to. Therefore, we stand firm by remembering what Jesus paid for by His blood (Ephesians 1:7; 1 Corinthians 6:20). We stand firm by focusing on the prize (Philippians 3:14). We stand firm by eagerly awaiting the promise of our Savior, who will redeem our bodies and bring us into His kingdom (Titus 2:13). We cannot comprehend how much greater the prize will be. No matter how difficult the road may become, stay the course! Stick to the fight! Keep your eyes on the prize.

Remember the metaphor of the woman in labor I talked about in chapter 3? She is an example of someone who is willing to suffer in order to obtain the prize set before her. Jesus also uses her as an example. He says, "A woman giving birth to a child has pain because her time has come; but when her baby is born she forgets the anguish because of her joy that a child is born into the world. So with you: Now is your time of grief, but I will see you again and you will rejoice, and no one will take away your joy" (John 16:21-22, emphasis mine).

Consider Him who endured such opposition from sinners,
so that you will not grow weary and lose heart.
(Hebrews 12:3, emphasis mine)

You need to *persevere so that* when you have done
the will of God, *you will receive what He*
has promised. For, "In just a little while,
He who is coming will come and will not delay."
(Hebrews 10:36–37, emphasis mine)

I eagerly expect and hope that *I will in no way be ashamed,*
but will have sufficient courage so that now as always Christ will
be exalted in my body, *whether by life or by death.*
(Philippians 1:20, emphasis added)

Fortitude in Persecution

Death cannot kill a believer, it can only usher
him into a freer form of life. [2]

~ C.H. Spurgeon

Webster defines *fortitude* as "the strength of mind that enables a person to encounter danger, bear pain, or adversity with courage". When I think of this word fortitude, I think of the millions of martyrs down through the centuries. I think of their courage in the face of torture and death. Fortitude can only exist in the soil of anticipation, which is nourished by focusing on the eternal reward rather than the physical.

No matter how serious the persecution becomes, the worst thing anyone can do to us is take our life. But is that even a bad thing? The Bible tells us that death here means life there (John 5:24; 11:25). Jesus has already taken the sting out of death (1 Corinthians 15:54-56). He has triumphed over death (Colossians 2:15, Acts 2:24). He has given us victory over death (1 Corinthians 15:57). And Paul tells us that to die is to gain Christ (Philippians 1:21). This is why the martyrs had the fortitude to stand strong. They saw their eternal reward just within reach.

The LORD is with me; I will not be afraid.
What can mere mortals do to me?
(Psalms 118:6, emphasis added)

Blessed are those who are persecuted because of
righteousness, for theirs is the kingdom of heaven. *Blessed are*
you when people insult you, persecute you and falsely
say all kinds of evil against you because of me.
(Matthew 5:10-11, emphasis mine)

*Do not be afraid of those who kill the
body but cannot kill the soul.*
(Matthew 10:28, emphasis added)

Blessed is the one who perseveres under trial because,
having stood the test, *that person will receive the crown of life*
that the Lord has promised to those who love Him.
(James 1:12, emphasis mine)

*If you are insulted because of the name
of Christ, you are blessed,* for the
Spirit of glory and of God rests on you.
(1 Peter 4:14, emphasis added)

Be faithful unto death, and I will give you the crown of life.
(Revelation 2:10, ESV, emphasis added)

Conclusion

In order to receive the most joy from our gift of suffering, we must learn how to handle it properly. Our "user guide" – the Word of God – tells us that our hope, joy, attitude, perspective, anticipation, and fortitude are how we are to handle this gift (Philippians 1:29). Without these applications, we will not be able to appreciate or utilize our gift adequately. While enduring our trials, it is important to search our hearts often, making sure our attitudes are in check and grounded in our future hope.

――――――― ⁑ ―――――――

*Therefore, since Christ suffered in His body, arm
yourselves also with the same attitude.*

1 PETER 4:1

Wrapped with a Bow:
The Promises of God

Throughout history, God has demonstrated that He is supremely trustworthy. That's why, in one sense, nothing could be more foolish than not to trust in the promises of God. [1]

~ R.C. Sproul

Now that we've inspected the box that holds our gift, examined the contents of this gift, and have read the user guide that instructs our attitudes, I want to finish by watching God wrap our gift box with the big, bright, beautiful crimson bow of His promises.

When we think of scripture verses that speak of God's promises in our suffering, I would venture to say that Romans 8:28 is probably one of the first verses that comes to mind. It is probably one of the most memorized and quoted verses among Christians. But in case you aren't familiar with it, this is what it says:

And we know that in all things God works for the good of those who love Him, who have been called according to His purpose.

The first phrase, "and we know", is a statement of irrefutable certainty that we, the ones who have been called according to His purpose, have a promise from God. I watched a sermon by Dr. David Jeremiah a while back on the topic of Romans 8:28. In his sermon, he gave us five promises that are found within this verse. They are:

1. A definite promise - *"And we know"*
2. A definitive promise - *"that in all things"*
3. A divine promise - *"God works"*
4. A dynamic promise - *"for the good"*
5. A defined promise - *"of those who love Him, who have been called according to His purpose"*

It is *only* because of God's kind and loving promises that we have any foundation to trust Him and His sovereignty through our suffering, let alone have the ability to delight in God's purposes for them. However, of all the beautiful promises we find in God's Word, the promise that our suffering will never be wasted should be the first one we use to strengthen our trust, faith, and joy through our trials.

I can't emphasize enough how important it is to hide God's Word in our hearts. Corrie Ten Boom once said, "Gather the riches of God's promises. Nobody can take away from you those texts from the Bible which you have learned by heart." Meditating on the promises we find in His word is the only way we can find the full assurance of our hope. I want us to be as uplifted as David was when he said:

My comfort in my suffering is this: Your promise preserves my life.
(Psalm 119:50, emphasis mine)

Trustworthy and Faithful

*Teach me your way, LORD, that I
may rely on your faithfulness.*

PSALM 86:11

There are three reasons why we can know for certain that God is trustworthy. They are:

1. God is trustworthy because He is not like us. We fail. We break promises, not just to each other, but also to God. We cannot be dependable or reliable all of the time. Even the most honorable person you know will disappoint and default on their commitments. We can all try to live our best, but we are only human. However, God is not! Numbers 23:19 says, "God is not human, that He should lie, not a human being, that He should change His mind. Does He speak and then not act? Does He promise and not fulfill?"

2. God is trustworthy because He is unchanging. On the other hand, we are often indecisive, and waver in our convictions. James tells us that the person who doubts is like a wave tossed by the wind (James 1:6), and in contrast, he tells us that God "does not change like shifting shadows" (James 1:17). In addition to James, the writer of Hebrews tells us that He is "the same yesterday and today and forever" (Hebrews 13:8).

3. God is trustworthy because He is infinitely wise. He knows the end from the beginning (Isaiah 46:10). He isn't making things up on the fly, and He doesn't need to make adjustments, alterations, or amendments to His plan as He goes. Nothing that happens takes Him by surprise. His purpose will stand, and no other purpose could be superior.

The LORD will fulfill His purpose for me.
(Psalm 138:8, ESV, emphasis mine)

The LORD is *trustworthy in all He promises*
and *faithful in all He does.*
(Psalm 145:13, emphasis mine)

He is the Maker of heaven and earth, the sea,
and everything in them – *He remains faithful forever.*
(Psalm 146:6, emphasis mine)

God is faithful, who has called you into
fellowship with His Son, Jesus Christ our Lord.
(1 Corinthians 1:9, emphasis mine)

I like what Matthew Henry's Concise Commentary on Psalm 116:10-19 says about this topic of God's faithfulness and our faithlessness.

> Yet there may be true faith where there are workings of unbelief; but then faith will prevail; and being humbled for our distrust of God's word, we shall experience his faithfulness to it. What can the pardoned sinner, or what can those who have been delivered from trouble or distress, render to the Lord for his benefits? We cannot in any way profit him. Our best is unworthy of his acceptance; yet we ought to devote ourselves and all we have to his service. [2]

Reminding God of His Promises

I don't know about you, but I often get weary of repeatedly asking for God's help. Waiting for Him to answer is hard, especially when it doesn't seem like He is listening. He can feel so far away and I often act as though He's forgotten me. It's difficult to be hopeful when my prayers aren't being answered (or at least, the way I would like to have them answered), and I often want to give up. I think that's why I like reading the Psalms so much. I feel David's loneliness in his physical, mental, and emotional distress. Like me, he is continually crying out and asking God why He has forsaken him, asking why he feels alone and abandoned by Him. He never comes to God with the attempt of hiding what he's feeling and he's not too proud to admit that he is overwhelmed.

> All my longings lie open before you, Lord; my sighing is not
> hidden from you. My heart pounds, my strength fails me;
> even the light has gone from my eyes.
> (Psalm 38:9-10).

However, as David is pouring himself out to God, he not only reminds himself of God's promises, but he continues to remind God also (Psalm 70 and 86). It is when we find ourselves in times of loneliness and hopelessness that we must press in even deeper, not only to remind ourselves, but to also remind God of His promise to draw near to us. Do not be too proud to ask Him to give you His comfort and peace, to deliver, strengthen and help you in your time of need. It takes humility to be open and honest when our strength is growing thin. Remember, it brings Him glory when we remind Him of His promises. In doing so, we are truly showing God that we are aware of them and are trusting in them. And when we align our prayers with His promises, it invites us and others to proclaim the glory and splendor of our King.

The 23rd chapter of Job pictures him desperately seeking to find God.

> If only I knew where to find Him;
> if only I could go to His dwelling!
> (Job 23:3)

However, just 10 verses down we get a sense of Job's awe-stricken fear of God.

> But He stands alone, and who can oppose Him?
> He does whatever He pleases. He carries out His decree
> against me, and many such plans He still has in store.
> That is why I am terrified before Him; when I think of all
> this, I fear Him. God has made my heart faint;
> the Almighty has terrified me.
> (Job 23:13-16)

Nonetheless, despite God's dreadful, awesome, power and sovereignty, Job also knew the love and kindness of God. Finding Him was all Job wanted. He knew he would still be safer with God than without Him. I like these words Charles Spurgeon uses:

> God's children run home when the storm comes
> on. It is the heaven-born instinct of a gracious soul
> to seek shelter from all ills beneath the wings of
> Jehovah. "He that hath made his refuge God,"
> might serve as the title of a true believer. [3]

When we are overwhelmed with hopelessness and despair, why would we run anywhere else when we have the Lord Jesus Christ who bought us with a price? He defeated sin and death (Hebrews 2:14) and is in control of *everything* (Psalm 22:28; Colossians 1:17). We will only find emptiness outside of our faithful Father. So when God weighs down His children with suffering, we must not resent the affliction, but instead, accept it and seek refuge in the One who has ordained it.

So, what are you struggling with today? Is your flesh fragile? Is your spirit weak? Are your circumstances being challenged? Do you feel as though your comfort is gone? Cry out to Him. Don't hesitate to pour yourself and be honest about how you feel. He *does* care and He wants to listen to your heart's cry. So insist that He come to your aid. God is not offended by it. He even tells us to do it. He says, "Put Me in remembrance…" (Isaiah 43:26, NASB), and "You who call on the LORD, give yourselves no rest, and give Him no rest…" (Isaiah 62:6-7).

And if you don't know how to pray, use the inspired prayers God gave to us in His Word. He gave them to us so we don't have to come up with our own when we are stuck. It's like an open book test. We don't have to have all the answers because He's already given them to us. Here are just a handful of examples:

> *Have mercy on me, LORD*, for I am faint; heal me, LORD,
> for my bones are in agony. My soul is in deep anguish.
> *How long, LORD*, how long? Turn, LORD, and *deliver me*;
> *save me because of your unfailing love.*
> (Psalm 6:2-4, emphasis mine)

> Those who know your name trust in you, for *you,*
> *LORD, have never forsaken* those who seek you.
> *He does not ignore the cries* of the afflicted.
> (Psalm 9:10 & 12, emphasis mine)

> You, LORD, *hear the desire of the afflicted*;
> you encourage them, and *you listen to their cry.*
> (Psalm 10:17, emphasis mine)

> Since you are my rock and my fortress,
> *for the sake of your name lead and guide me.*
> (Psalm 31:3, emphasis mine)

> *LORD, do not forsake me; do not be far from me*, my God.
> *Come quickly to help me*, my Lord and my Savior.
> (Psalm 38:21–22, emphasis mine)

Answer me, LORD, out of the goodness of your love;
in your great mercy *turn to me. Do not hide your face* from
your servant; *answer me quickly*, for *I am in trouble.*
(Psalm 69:16-17, emphasis mine)

Help us, God our Savior, *for the glory of your name;*
deliver us and forgive our sins *for your name's sake.*
(Psalm 79:9, emphasis mine)

For this is what the high and exalted One says – He who lives forever,
whose name is holy: *"I live in a high and holy place, but also with*
the one who is contrite and lowly in spirit, to revive the spirit of the
lowly and to revive the heart of the contrite."
(Isaiah 57:15, emphasis mine)

For the eyes of the Lord are on the righteous,
and *His ears are attentive to their prayer.*
(1 Peter 3:12, emphasis mine)

The Lord knows how to rescue the godly from trials.
(2 Peter 2:9, emphasis mine)

The Promise of Peace and His Presence

Nowhere in the Bible does it talk about the absence of calamity for
believers. Instead, we see the very opposite (Job 5:7). But the most
reassuring thing we do read, over and over, is God's promise of
His presence in our lives, *especially* in our trials and tragedies. One
of my favorite statements Moses gave to the Israelites is found in
Deuteronomy 4:7. He states, "What other nation is so great as to
have their gods near them the way the LORD our God is near us
whenever we pray to Him?"

Another one of my favorite examples of God's presence with
His people is found in Joseph's story. Genesis chapter 39 tells the

portion of his story while he was in Egypt. He was sold as a slave, falsely accused, and thrown into prison. Yet, the phrase "The Lord was with Joseph" is stated four times just within this chapter alone. It was God's faithful presence that was Joseph's anchor through his trials.

Here are some more of my favorite verses that assure me of this promise in my times of trouble.

I have told you these things, so that *in me you may have peace*. In this world you will have trouble. But take heart! I have overcome the world.
(John 16:33, emphasis mine)

God has said, *"Never will I leave you; never will I forsake you."*
(Hebrews 13:5, emphasis mine)

Peace I leave with you; *my peace I give you.* I do not give to you as the world gives. *Do not* let your hearts *be troubled* and *do not be afraid."*
(John 14:27, emphasis mine)

The LORD Himself goes before you and *will be with you; He will never leave you nor forsake you.* Do not be afraid; do not be discouraged.
(Deuteronomy 31:8, emphasis mine)

So do not fear, for *I am with you;* do not be dismayed, for I am your God.
(Isaiah 41:10, emphasis mine)

When you pass through the waters, I will be with you; and *when you pass through the rivers, they will not sweep over you.*

When you walk through the fire, you will not be burned;
    the flames will not set you ablaze.
    (Isaiah 43:2, emphasis mine)

Note how God talks about our trials in the verse above through the prophet Isaiah. We are *not* told that we are going to be delivered out of our troubles, but rather through them. It speaks to *when*, not *if* you pass through the waters, rivers, and fire. These things *will* come. However, we have God's assurance of His presence and, eventually, our deliverance through them. We may not see the deliverance, especially how and when we would like to see it, but nevertheless, God is faithful and true. We can trust His promise when He tells us that He will be with us and will deliver us. In this quote below, Timothy Keller talks about knowing God as He walks through the fire with us:

> Suffering can refine us rather than destroy us because God himself walks with us in the fire.... We must recognize, depend on, speak with, and believe in God while in the fire...Knowing Him personally while in our affliction is the key to becoming stronger rather than weaker in it. [4]

The Promise of Deliverance, Restoration, and Help

I like this quote from Lindsey Tollefson taken from her book *Psalms for trials: Meditations of Praying the Psalms*: "[God] delights to deliver. Sometimes His deliverance brings us out of our storm, and sometimes His deliverance meets us with grace in the storm." [5] Here's another good quote from John Piper: "The gospel is not a 'help wanted' sign. It is a 'help available' sign." [6]

Here are some scriptures you can refer to when you need to be reminded of His promise to deliver, bring restoration, and to help us in our time of need.

He restores my soul; He guides me in the
paths of righteousness *For His name's sake.*
(Psalm 23:3, NASB, emphasis mine)

The angel of the LORD encamps around
those who fear Him, and *He delivers them.*
(Psalm 34:7, emphasis mine)

The righteous cry out, and *the LORD hears them;*
He *delivers them* from all their troubles.
The LORD *is close to the brokenhearted* and
saves those who are crushed in spirit.
(Psalm 34:17-18, emphasis mine)

Call on me in the day of trouble;
I will deliver you, and you will honor me.
(Psalm 50:15, emphasis mine)

He will call on me, and *I will answer
him;* I will *be with him in trouble,*
I will *deliver him* and *honor him.*
(Psalm 91:15, emphasis mine)

I lift up my eyes to the mountains — where
does my help come from? *My help comes from
the LORD,* the Maker of heaven and earth.
(Psalm 121:1-2, emphasis mine)

I will strengthen you and help you;
I will uphold you with my righteous right hand.
(Isaiah 41:10, emphasis mine)

For I am the LORD your God *who takes hold of your right hand* and says to you, Do not fear; *I will help you.*
(Isaiah 41:13, emphasis mine)

Since ancient times no one has heard, no ear has perceived, no eye has seen any *God* besides you, who *acts on behalf of those who wait for Him.*
(Isaiah 64:4, emphasis mine)

God is just: He will pay back trouble to those who trouble you and *give relief* to you who are troubled, and to us as well.
(2 Thessalonians 1:6-7, emphasis mine)

The Lord will rescue me from every evil attack *and will bring me safely* to His heavenly kingdom.
(2 Timothy 4:18, emphasis mine)

And the God of all grace, who called you to His eternal glory in Christ, after you have suffered a little while, *will Himself restore you and make you strong, firm and steadfast.*
(1 Peter 5:10, emphasis mine)

He has delivered us from such a deadly peril, and *He will deliver us* again. On Him we have set our hope that *He will continue to deliver us.*
(2 Corinthians 1:10, emphasis mine)

I love this last verse in 2 Corinthians. God *has* delivered us. God *will* deliver us. God *continues* to deliver us. This is what past, present, and future grace looks like.

The Promise of Protection and Strength

Here are some scripture you can refer to when you need to be reminded of His promise to protect you and to strengthen as you walk through your trials.

The LORD will fight for you; you need only to be still.
(Exodus 14:14, emphasis mine)

The LORD is my strength and my defense;
He has become my salvation.
(Exodus 15:2, emphasis mine)

For *the eyes of the LORD range throughout
the earth to strengthen those* whose
hearts are fully committed to Him.
(2 Chronicles 16:9, emphasis mine)

Do not grieve, for *the joy
of the LORD is your strength*.
(Nehemiah 8:10, emphasis mine)

The LORD is my strength and my shield;
my heart trusts in Him, and He helps me.
(Psalm 28:7, emphasis mine)

God is our refuge and strength,
an *ever-present help in trouble*.
(Psalm 46:1, emphasis mine)

He will not let your foot slip – He
who watches over you will not slumber.
(Psalm 121:3, emphasis mine)

For *He guards the course* of the just and
protects the way of His faithful ones.
(Proverbs 2:8, emphasis mine)

Every word of God is flawless; *He is a
shield* to those who take refuge in Him.
(Proverbs 30:5, emphasis mine)

He gives strength to the weary
and increases the power of the weak.
(Isaiah 40:29, emphasis mine)

*No weapon forged against you will prevail…
This is the heritage* of the servants of the LORD.
(Isaiah 54:17, emphasis mine)

The LORD is good, a *refuge in times of
trouble*. He cares for those who trust in Him.
(Nahum 1:7, emphasis mine)

But *the Lord is faithful*, and *He will strengthen
you and protect you* from the evil one.
(2 Thessalonians 3:3, emphasis mine)

The Promise of His Love, Comfort, and Compassion

We often don't feel the love of our Father. But that's not His fault
when we don't. That's on us for not "calling to mind" the love He
has promised us (Lamentations 3:21-22). I hope the scriptures below
will help you fight off the lies of the enemy. Remember, bookend
each of Satan's lies with two promises of God. Remind yourself that
God is a good Father, a God of compassion, and a place of refuge
and comfort for the brokenhearted.

This is love: not that we loved God, but that
He loved us and sent His Son as an atoning sacrifice for our sins.
And so *we know and rely on the love God has for us.*
(1 John 4:10 & 16, emphasis mine)

But *because of His great love for us*, God, who is rich in mercy,
made us alive with Christ even when we were dead in transgression.
(Ephesians 2:4-5, emphasis mine)

Praise be to the God and Father of our Lord Jesus Christ, the Father
of compassion and the God of all comfort, *who comforts us in all our
troubles*…so also *our comfort abounds through Christ*.
(2 Corinthians 1:3-5, emphasis mine)

But when *the Comforter* is come, whom I will send unto
you from the Father, *even the Spirit of truth, which
proceedeth from the Father,* He shall testify of me.
(John 15:26, KJV, emphasis mine)

The LORD your God is with you, the Mighty Warrior who saves.
*He will take great delight in you; in His love He will no
longer rebuke you, but will rejoice over you with singing.*
(Zephaniah 3:17, emphasis mine)

"Though the mountains be shaken and the hills be removed, yet *my
unfailing love for you will not be shaken* nor my covenant of
peace be removed", says the LORD, who has compassion on you.
(Isaiah 54:10, emphasis mine)

Yet *the LORD longs to be gracious to you;*
therefore *He will rise up to show you compassion.*
(Isaiah 30:18, emphasis mine)

Though He brings grief, *He will show
compassion*, so *great is His unfailing love*.
(Lamentations 3:32, emphasis mine)

Even though I walk through the darkest valley, I will fear no evil,
for y*ou are with me; your rod and your staff, they comfort me*.
(Psalm 23:4, emphasis mine)

The LORD's unfailing love surrounds the one who trusts in Him.
(Psalm 32:10, emphasis mine)

But *you, LORD, are a compassionate and gracious God*,
slow to anger, abounding in love and faithfulness.
(Psalm 86:15, emphasis mine)

Give me a sign of your goodness... *For you,
LORD, have* helped me and *comforted me*.
(Psalm 86:17, emphasis mine)

As a father has compassion on his children, so *the
LORD has compassion on those who fear Him*; for He knows
how we are formed, He remembers that we are dust.
(Psalm 103:13-14, emphasis mine)

May your unfailing love be my comfort,
according to your promise to your servant.
(Psalm 119:76, emphasis mine)

*You have kept count of my tossings;
put my tears in your bottle*.
Are they not in your book?...
This I know, that God is for me.
(Psalm 56:8-9, ESV, emphasis mine)

God is keeping count of our tossing's. He puts our tears in His bottle. Our suffering is recorded in His book. These are all statements that show how tenderhearted and compassionate our Father is toward us.

Beauty for Ashes

In the summer of '96, only 6 months after we lost Tyler and my Oma, and while we were watching Phil's mother fade away, I was driving home after visiting with her for the afternoon. While I was driving I heard a song come on the radio. It was *Beauty for Ashes* by Crystal Lewis. It overwhelmed me so much that I had to pull the car over on the side of the road. These are the words to the chorus: "He gives beauty for ashes. Strength for fear. Gladness for mourning. Peace for despair." [7]

The message of this song is found in Isaiah 61:3. Interestingly enough, the two verses above verse 3 happen to be the portion of Isaiah that Jesus stood up to read at the synagogue in Nazareth, His hometown. Let's look at what Isaiah writes under the inspiration of the Holy Spirit.

> The Spirit of the Sovereign LORD is on me, because the LORD has anointed me to proclaim good news to the poor. He has sent me to bind up the brokenhearted, to proclaim freedom for the captives and release from darkness for the prisoners, to proclaim the year of the LORD's favor, and the day of vengeance of our God, *to comfort all who mourn, and provide for those who grieve in Zion – to bestow on them a crown of beauty instead of ashes, the oil of joy instead of mourning, and a garment of praise instead of a spirit of despair.* They will be called oaks of righteousness, a planting of the LORD for the display of His splendor. (Isaiah 61:1-3, emphasis added)

Even though the gospel of Luke only records Jesus reading a portion of this passage above (Luke 4:18-19), Jesus is naturally pointing out that this *whole* passage in Isaiah is about Him. He was publicly telling His listeners that He was their Messiah, that He had finally come to release those who were spiritual prisoners and captives to their sin. But that wasn't all. He was also telling them that He came for the brokenhearted. He came for those who were grieving and mourning. He came for those who found themselves in despair. He isn't just the Messiah of the world. He is a personal Messiah for every individual who puts their trust in Him.

Above all else, Jesus brings freedom to His people by saving them from their sin. Additionally, He takes away their ashes and gives them a crown of beauty. He takes away their mourning and gives them His oil of joy. He takes away their spirit of despair and gives them His garment of praise.

I felt as though I was in a puddle of "ashes and despair" as I was driving home that day. I was barely holding it together. Then God dropped this song right into my lap. He stepped into my life that day, not just as the Savior of my soul, but as a personal Savior who shared my pain and who came to exchange it for His joy and for His beauty. This is what He came for: His people — each and every one of us. He meets us where we are, He walks with us through our pain, and He turns our ashes into beautiful things.

The Promise Preservation

If there be one stitch in the celestial garment of our righteousness which we are to insert ourselves, then we are lost; but this is our confidence, the Lord who began will perfect. He has done it all, must do it all, and will do it all. [8]

~ C.H. Spurgeon

One of my favorite Biblical doctrines is called the *Preservation of the Saints,* or as some prefer to call it, the *Perseverance of the Saints.* The idea behind this doctrine is that those who are born again are guaranteed eternal security. (I personally like *Preservation of the Saints* because it puts the emphases on God doing the preservation as opposed to man doing any amount of persevering.) However, the name given to any doctrine is not what matters as long as the topic matter is accurate with what the Bible teaches.

This doctrine of eternal security can be a little tricky for some people. I can't tell you how many times I've heard the question, "How can I know if I am truly saved?" I have even struggled with the anxieties and uncertainties of my own salvation in the past. Even though there are numerous scripture verses that teach this doctrine of the Perseverance of the Saints, there are a few scripture verses that seem to be talking about falling from grace, or losing salvation. At one point in my life, I let these few verses override the multiple ones that gave me certainty of my eternal security. However, when I finally learned how to read and interpret them in context, I found that these people who "fall away from the faith" (Galatians 5:4), or who "can't be brought back to repentance" (Hebrews 6:4-6), were never really saved to begin with. If someone shows signs of conversion and then walks away, or if they have professed faith yet do not live like they have, then their conversion was a false one. John tells us that they were never one of us (1 John 2:19). Jesus Himself taught that not everyone who professes to believe is truly saved (Matthew 7:21-22).

So how do we know if we are truly saved? Well, the Bible teaches us that if we do confess Jesus as Lord, then we must continually test our salvation (2 Corinthians 13:5; 2 Peter 1:10) and examine our lives to make sure we are growing in godliness (Philippians 2:12-13). We can be assured of our salvation in this way: if we regard Christ as highly esteemed and our concern is how we might honor Him with our lives, and if we search for

Him with sincerity of heart and believe there is nothing we can do to add to the work of Christ, then His grace has had its effect on us and our eternal security is assured. And so we fix "our eyes on Jesus, *the author and perfecter of faith*" (Hebrews 12:2, NASB, emphasis mine).

God gives us His Holy Spirit who indwells within us as a guarantee that we will not lose our salvation (Ephesians 1:13-14; 2 Corinthians 1:22). This is a promise, and God cannot go back on His promises (Numbers 23:19). Therefore, the believer is eternally secure because God is eternally faithful.

For God's *gifts and His call are irrevocable*.
(Romans 11:29, emphasis mine)

He will also keep you firm to the end, so that you
will be blameless on the day of our Lord Jesus Christ.
God is faithful, who has called you into fellowship
with his Son, Jesus Christ our Lord.
(1 Corinthians 1:8-9, emphasis mine)

May God Himself, the God of peace,
sanctify you through and through.
May your whole spirit, soul and body *be*
kept blameless at the coming of
our Lord Jesus Christ. *The one who calls*
you is faithful, and He will do it.
(1 Thessalonians 5:23-24; emphasis mine)

[I] am convinced that *He is able to guard*
what I have entrusted to Him until that day.
(2 Timothy 1:12, emphasis mine)

And this is what *He promised us — eternal life*.
(1 John 2:25, emphasis mine)

It is only God who can begin this *good work* in us. This work is our regeneration, the point at which our salvation is applied. If we have bowed our knees to Christ, then we have this assurance: He has saved us, and therefore He will carry this work of salvation to completion. Another one of my favorite verses, that speaks of this assurance, is Philippians 1:6. It says:

> Being confident of this, that *He who began a good work in you will carry it on to completion until the day of Christ Jesus.*
> (emphasis mine)

When God shakes His people, it can be painful and sometimes seem harsh, yet He has promised that not one of His beloved children will fall to the ground to be lost (Amos 9:9). Jesus told His disciples that He would lose *none* that the Father has given Him (John 6:39). Every single one of His believers are precious in His sight.

They say that if you get a tattoo you should never put a significant other's name on you, because if they happen to become insignificant, then you are stuck with that name forever marking your body. However, in Isaiah, God tells His chosen people: "See, I have engraved you on the palms of my hands" (Isaiah 49:16). Remember, we break promises, but God never will. This "engraving on the palms of His hands" signifies that we cannot, will not, *ever*, be removed from His love or eternal security.

> Who shall separate us from the love of Christ? Shall trouble or hardship or persecution or famine or nakedness or danger or sword? For I am convinced that neither death nor life, neither angels nor demons, neither the present nor the future, nor any powers, neither height nor depth, ***nor anything else in all creation, will be able to separate us from the love of God*** that is in Christ Jesus our Lord.
> (Romans 8:35, 38-39; emphasis mine)

This verse tells us two things regarding our preservation. First, no one can bring accusation against God's chosen people. And second, nothing in all of creation can separate His people from the love of Christ. I like how R.C. Sproul talked about our promise of perseverance. He stated:

> We are able to persevere only because God works within us, within our free wills. And because God is at work in us, we are certain to persevere. The decrees of God concerning election are immutable. They do not change, because He does not change. All whom He justifies He glorifies. None of the elect has ever been lost. [9]

Conclusion

We break our promises. It's what we do as fallen, sinful man. However, despite our unfaithfulness, we serve a God who will never break His. He may not grant every request, but He has promised His presence and His comfort. He doesn't always grant deliverance from our pain, but He does promise His deliverance through it. We are under God's providential care, and He is bigger than our burdens.

As we've continued to learn, God will be faithful to fulfill His purposes in us, and one of the means by which He uses to accomplish them is the gift of our suffering. Because it is a gift, God's people will survive any trial, knowing it is wrapped with the bow of His promises. It is wrapped with His presence, His peace, His deliverance and restoration. It is wrapped with His promise of help, protection, strength, and His love and comfort. Last of all, it's wrapped with His promise of preserving us as we walk through the fire. Remember: "He gives beauty for ashes. Strength for fear. Gladness for mourning. Peace for despair."

————————— ++++++ ——————————

For no matter how many promises God has made, they are "Yes" in Christ. And so through Him the "Amen" is spoken by us to the glory of God.

2 CORINTHIANS 1:20

The Gift of All Gifts

Every good and perfect gift is from above, coming down from the Father of the heavenly lights, who does not change like shifting shadows.

~ JAMES 1:17

God has perfectly fashioned our gift of suffering, and as we have witnessed through His inspired Word, we know He has assigned a high value upon it. We find this gift contained within the box of His sovereignty and wrapped with the bow of His promises. I hope by now you have gained a sufficient understanding of this Biblical approach to understanding why we suffer and why it is a gift. But ultimately, I pray that your anticipation of this remarkable gift, and what it leads to, has increasingly flourished in your spirit. It is the Gift of all gifts: our eternal life with our beautiful Savior, Jesus Christ! This is where true life will begin.

Paul tells us that God has first given us the gift to believe in Jesus, then He has given us the gift to suffer for Him. So, if you have believed in your heart and have confessed with your mouth that Jesus is the Lord of your life (Romans 10:9-10), if you have surrendered your own efforts to be worthy of God and have accepted Christ's work on your behalf (Titus 3:5, Romans 3:24-25), then you have been called to receive this gift (1 Timothy 6:12). Romans 8:30 says, "And those He predestined, He also called; those He called, He also justified; those He justified, He also glorified." This is His promise: there is *justification* for those of us who have been *called* to be God's children, and there is *glorification* for those of us who have been *justified*. The final chapter of our redemption will be our own glorification.

Now if *we are children*, then we are heirs - heirs *of God and co-heirs with Christ*, if indeed *we share in His sufferings in order that we may also share in His glory*. I consider that our present sufferings are not worth comparing with the glory that will be revealed in us.
(Romans 8:17-18, emphasis mine)

Each one of us has a story (Psalm 138:16). Mine might look different from yours, and yours might be more tragic than mine. Nevertheless, God has written each one of them, and He has placed purpose behind every ounce of pain found upon our pages. However, not only has He ordained our trials, He has also put limits to them. We have the promise that we are not outside of His sovereign control. Because of this, we should be able to trust Him with our pain. I love this quote from Charles Spurgeon:

The God of providence has limited the time, manner, intensity, repetition, and effects of all our sicknesses; each throb is decreed, each sleepless hour predestined, each relapse ordained, each depression of spirit foreknown, and each sanctifying result eternally purposed. [1]

It is Well With My Soul

Have you ever read the story of Horatio G. Spafford, the man who wrote the well-loved hymn, *It is Well With My Soul*? Ever since reading it for myself, his faith has truly been a model for my own.

Horatio Spafford was a successful attorney and real estate investor who lost a fortune in the devastating Chicago Fire of 1871. Around the same time, his four-year-old son died of scarlet fever.

Thinking a vacation would be good for his family, he sent his wife and four daughters on a ship to England. He planned to join them after finishing some crucial business at home. Yet while his family was crossing the Atlantic, their ship collided with another ship and sank. More than 200 people lost their lives, including all four of Horatio's daughters. However, his wife Anna was among those who survived the tragedy. Once she arrived in England, she sent a telegram to her husband stating, "Saved alone, what shall I do?"

Horatio immediately set sail for England. During his voyage, the captain of the ship, who was aware of the tragedy, summoned Horatio to tell him that they were passing over the spot where the shipwreck had occurred. As Horatio thought about his daughters, he began to write these words of comfort.

> When peace like a river attendeth my way
> When sorrows like sea billows roll
> Whatever my lot, Thou has taught me to say
> It is well, it is well with my soul
>
> Though Satan should buffet,
> Though trials should come
> Let this blest assurance control
> That Christ has regarded my helpless estate
> And has shed his own blood for my soul

My sin, oh the bliss of this glorious thought
My sin, not in part, but the whole
Is nailed to the cross, and I bear it no more
Praise the Lord, praise the Lord, O my soul!

It is well
With my soul
It is well, it is well with my soul. [2]

There is an important lesson we can find in these lyrics. Horatio had concluded that all the insurmountable pain and suffering he had endured within such a short period of time was nothing in comparison to the devastation of being separated from God for eternity. He expressed his utmost gratitude for God's ultimate gift of salvation through the blood of Jesus Christ, even in the midst of feeling crushed by his losses. His physical being was in ruins yet his soul was secure in Christ, and that was what mattered the most.

A good friend and mentor of mine, upon seeing me, often asks not "How are you doing?", but rather "How is your soul?" My answer: "It is well!" The reason this is so impactful is because of the reminder it gives me. No matter how bad my day is going, or how much pain I'm in, or how my body is fighting against me, it is nothing in comparison to the security of my soul which has been given to me through the blood of Jesus.

I once read this analogy from a 16th-century theologian that has stuck with me. "As the spring accompanies the winter, so does glory follow our affliction. And as winter prepares the ground for spring, so does our suffering prepare us for glory." Just as the mother in labor and the athlete in rigorous training viewed their past pain worthy of their prize, we too will look back and consider our cost worth the glory. However, unlike their temporal and fading prize, our reward will be eternal and incorruptible (1 Peter 1:4). So when God has thoroughly finished His work in us, we will awaken to the face of Jesus of whom we have been conformed. This is why David could say:

> Precious in the sight of the LORD is
> the death of His faithful servants.
> (Psalm 116:15)

> Yet I am always with you; you hold me by my
> right hand. You guide me with your counsel,
> and *afterward you will take me into glory*.
> (Psalm 73:23-24, emphasis mine)

When God called Abraham out of his homeland, He proclaimed that He Himself was Abraham's "very great reward" (Genesis 15:1). God was telling Abraham that, above all the other promises He had given, His presence, His favor, and His blessings were the greatest of all. God is our reward too. He has given Himself to us through His Son, Jesus Christ.

Our joy takes place when we can see Him and Him alone, as all we need to satisfy our souls. It's good to ask God for our deliverance and for our healing. In fact, He has told us to do so. Nevertheless, we must also remember that if God chooses not to answer our prayers, for His own good purposes, there is no greater reward than Himself. One of my favorite verses is Psalm 73:25. It says, "Whom have I in heaven but you? And earth has nothing I desire besides you." Imagine how much more joy we could experience through our trials if the majority of our prayers were for God to give us more of Himself. And more of Him will only produce more anticipation for our hope of an eternity spent with Him. As Paul wrote to the Christians in Rome:

> I consider that *our present sufferings are not worth
> comparing with the glory* that will be revealed in us.
> (Romans 8:18, emphasis mine)

Remember in my introduction where I talked about how important it is to preach to yourself when you start feeling overwhelmed and resignation starts to worm its way in? Well, I've just given you every tool in my tool box. Now it's up to you to "call to mind" (Lamentations 3:21-22). The best weapon Satan's uses to destroy our hope is our forgetting of God's promises. But our best weapon is God's Word to not only remind us of them, but to also remind Satan.

God gave us His Word so we can know Him intimately, and we only get to know Him intimately when we begin to understand His character. If we don't know Him then we cannot worship Him in spirit and in truth (John 4:24). Knowing God and understanding His character is the only way we can love Him for who He truly is, without interjecting our own ideas of who or what He should be like. Let God speak for Himself. After all, He is the authority on His own character. He is the author and creator of our lives, and He uses every ounce of our pain for our good and for His glory. This is why our suffering is a gift. Let's start living like it is. And may we do it with joyful hope and anticipation for our ultimate gift: our eternal glory with Jesus Christ, our Lord.

--------- •┼♦♦┼• ---------

I pray that the eyes of your heart may be enlightened in order that you may know the hope to which He has called you, the riches of His glorious inheritance in His holy people, and His incomparably great power for us who believe.

EPHESIANS 1:18-19

To Him who is able to keep you from stumbling and to present you before His glorious presence without fault and with great joy — to the only God our Savior be glory, majesty, power and authority, through Jesus Christ our Lord, before all ages, now and forever more! Amen.

JUDE 24-25

Sola Deo gloria

Epilogue

If you did not consider yourself a follower of Christ when you picked this book up, and have finally landed on this last section, I applaud you. I'm sure you've been challenged many times along the way. You may have even put the book down with the intention of not picking it back up. Nevertheless, you're here. You made it through. Now what?

As you've probably made the connection by now, there is a big difference between the unbeliever and the Christian who has put their faith in the God of the Bible and His Son, Jesus Christ. But if you haven't figured it out by now, I'll tell you what it is. It's called HOPE.

You see, if someone believes there is no God, believes that Jesus is not the Savior, and/or believes the Bible is only a book of fairy tales, then what do they have that gives them comfort and tells them there is purpose and meaning behind their suffering? For the atheist who says, "There is no God!", life has no meaning. No ultimate purpose. Life exists only by chance and is randomly ordered. They live. They suffer. They die. They're gone. That's it.

If this is you (or was before reading this book), let's think about this a little more. Someone close to you dies. You lose a child. Your financial stability comes crashing down around you. You become sick with a fatal disease, or one for which there is no cure. Where is the purpose to any of this? Can you feel the weight of this emptiness? Do you feel the disconnect? Every individual wants meaning in their life, but how can there be meaning in a world without order? They want purpose to their life, but how can there be purpose outside of a Creator who creates and provides order?

If you want meaning and purpose to your life, there is only one way to get it.

Have you ever considered your life of sin? Oh, I can hear you now, "What? I don't live a life of sin! I'm a good person." Well, let me ask you another question. By what standard of good are you using to measure yourself? Because if you are not a believer in Christ yet, the only measure you have is your own arbitrary standard. We all have an arbitrary standard. But how many times do you even live up to your own standard of good? I know I can't. No one can live up to their own standard of what is good. But I'm not even talking about our own standard here. I'm talking about God's standard. The perfect, holy, and utmost righteous God who created the universe – who created you! It's His standard that we are measured against, and He says there is no one who is righteous (Romans 3:10-12) and that we all fall short of God's standards (Romans 3:23). Everyone (you and me included) has a sinful nature and corrupt desires (Ephesians 4:22-24). The Bible describes us as slaves to sin (Romans 6:17-18) and dead in our sin (Ephesians 2:1). It tells us that even our best efforts to be righteous are as rubbish (Philippians 3:7-10) and are like filthy rags to God (Isaiah 64:6).

No one will ever truly comprehend or appreciate the fullness of God's mercy — the Good News — this hope that belongs to the believer, unless we understand what His mercy saves us from — the bad news — His judgment and wrath on man's sin.

God has decreed that "the soul who sins will die" (Ezekiel 18:4, NASB). He is the standard of perfection, and no one lives up to it (Romans 3:23). We need to see God for who He is — God! "...His works are perfect, and all His ways are just. A faithful God who does no wrong, upright and just is He" (Deuteronomy 32:4). (See also Psalm 11:7). He created man and expects obedience (Exodus 20:4-6; Exodus 23:21; 2 John 6). When man disobeys God, man faces

God's wrath (Leviticus 26:14-18; Romans 1:18-32; Ephesians 2:3). Our sin stands against us to condemn us (Colossians 2:14), because of it we deserve God's wrath (Ephesians 2:3), and it earns us death (Romans 6:23). Furthermore, "God is a righteous judge, a God who displays His wrath every day. If He does not relent, He will sharpen His sword; He will bend and string His bow" (Psalm 7:11–12). Me? You? We are all in the crosshairs of His bow.

Now, let me ask you this. Have you ever thought about one day having to face a Holy God standing alone with only your sin to account for? What will be your excuse? What could possibly help you escape His judgment? Do you see it yet? Standing alone without hope for a chance that He will relent? You are lost. And if you remain where you are, you will fall under condemnation and there will never be any hope for an eternity spent in the presence of God. Instead, the Bible teaches that the unbeliever will go away to eternal punishment (Matthew 25:46, 2 Thessalonians 1:9), and perish unless he puts his faith in Jesus (John 3:16).

Now, here is the Good News. Because of God's love and mercy the Bible says that while we were still God's enemies - in the crosshairs of His bow - His Son, Jesus, died for our sins (Romans 5:8-10; Colossians 1:21). He took the wrath of God upon Himself so that we might be saved from it. I challenge you to read the whole chapter of Isaiah 53. It is the largest portion of Old Testament scripture detailing what the coming Messiah — Jesus Christ — would suffer for His people. In it, Isaiah prophesies that "He [Jesus] was pierced for our transgressions" and "He was crushed for our iniquities...Yet it was the LORD's will to crush Him and cause Him to suffer" and to make "His life an offering for sin" (Isaiah 53:5&10). He made atonement for our sins (Romans 3:24; 1 John 2:2; 4:10), which means He paid the price of death that we owed God, so we wouldn't have to.

According to the Bible, God is a holy and just God who will not, and cannot, tolerate sin. There must be punishment for the wrongs committed. Likewise, a just judge could never let a guilty person go without some form of retribution or punishment served for his crime, otherwise there would be no justice for the crime committed. So how can He acquit the guilty and yet not be guilty Himself in doing so?

One of my favorite words in the English language is impute. Impute is a legal term that means "to attach or ascribe. To place responsibility or blame on one person for acts of another person because of a particular relationship, such as mother to child, guardian to ward, employer to employee, or business associates".[1] The Bible uses this concept as well when talking about our sin and Jesus' righteousness. Except when speaking theologically about imputed righteousness, it's more than just crediting Jesus' righteousness to the Christian, enabling the Christian to be justified. There is a double imputation going on here. The believer's sin is also imputed to Jesus. He became sin for us so we could become righteous before God (2 Corinthians 5:21).

Think of it this way. We are in a courtroom. God is the Judge. We are the criminals who are being tried for our crimes. The wholly righteous and just Judge strikes the gavel on His bench to declare our guilt and give us our sentence of death. But just as He announces the verdict, Jesus, God's Son, steps in as our representative and tells the Judge that He will pay the punishment of our sins on our behalf — because justice must still be served for our crime. But Jesus doesn't stop there. He also gives us His perfect record so the Judge will let us go free. The Judge agrees. He assigns our sin, and the punishment for it, to His Son. Then the Judge credits His Son's righteousness to us. The Bible calls this being justified. This is one of my husband's favorite words - "justified". But he says it like this: "Just as if I'd never sinned".

Remember the definition of *imputation* above? God, our Just Judge, ascribes our punishment to Jesus and He (God) imputes Jesus' righteousness to us once we put our faith in Him (Jesus). Our sins are forgiven and we are justified before God. This is how God can uphold His justice and yet be merciful at the same time. He is

BOTH! The Just and the Justifier. So without Jesus, God's mercy on us would not be just. In fact there would be no mercy at all, *because* God is just. Judgment will be served. But if we put our faith in Jesus to cover the punishment for our sins, God's judgment passes over us. However, His judgment will fall upon the unbeliever who has not trusted in Christ.

In 2 Corinthians 5:21, Paul spells this out perfectly. He says, "God made Him who had no sin to be sin for us, so that in Him we might become the righteousness of God." He states this again in Romans 3:25-26. Paul says, "God presented Christ as a sacrifice of atonement, through the shedding of his blood - to be received by faith. He did this to demonstrate His righteousness, because in His forbearance He had left the sins committed beforehand unpunished – He did it to demonstrate His righteousness at the present time, so as to be just and the One who justifies those who have faith in Jesus."

The shame and rejection. The crown of thorns that pierced Jesus' head. The 39 lashes from the whip that caused the flesh to be torn from His back. The beatings that Jesus took. The nails in His hands and feet and the spear that pierced His side. That death – that should have been ours. We deserved His cross. But Jesus took our place. He gave us what we did not deserve and withheld from us what we did deserve. Jesus drank His own cup of wrath so that we wouldn't have to, if we accept it.

For the most part, the Bible is intended for the edification of believers. However, there is one consistent theme in it for unbelievers. It is the command to "Repent!" (Matthew 4:17; Luke 5:32; Acts 17:30; Acts 20:21). Jesus calls all sinners to repent (Luke 5:32). And if you do, you are promised new life in Christ. God assures us that if we seek Him we will find Him (Jeremiah 29:13; Matthew 7:8). Jesus says He won't cast out anyone who comes to Him (John 6:37). 1 John 1:9 says, "If we confess our sins, He is faithful and just and will forgive us our sins…". And if you repent and call out to Him, Jesus brings you to God (1 Peter 3:18), and then you have the promise of hope for an eternal life with Him (John 3:16).

I like how John Piper explains this:

> If the most terrifying news in the world is that we have fallen under the condemnation of our Creator and that He is bound by His own righteous character to preserve the worth of His glory by pouring out His wrath on our sin...then the best news in all the world (the gospel) is that God has decreed and enacted a way of salvation that also upholds the worth of His glory, the honor of His Son, and the eternal salvation of His elect. Jesus Christ came into the world to save sinners. [2]

Remember what I shared about the difference between believers and unbelievers? It was HOPE. Jesus is where our hope lies. It is because of this hope that we can find purpose in our suffering. When God and His word become the foundation for our life, we can stand firm knowing that our pain has meaning.

Have you ever had someone try to speak into your life who has never walked in your shoes? They have no qualification to speak to your pain because they don't have the ability to fully understand what you are going through. Sure, they can be sympathetic towards your pain, but they cannot be empathetic.

But Jesus? He doesn't just speak to us in our pain. He *meets* us in our pain. Jesus entered into His creation and suffered among us. He is qualified to meet us in every inch of our pain. He experienced the loss of loved ones. He knows what it feels like to have family members hate him. He knows what it's like to be abandoned by His closest friends. He was slandered unjustly. People were out for His life. He knows what it's like to have someone take your body and do things to it without your permission. Here is the most glorious thing – He did it for His people. This is why He is qualified to meet us in our pain.

Wouldn't you rather exchange the eternal suffering you deserve with temporary suffering that comes with a promise? Wouldn't it be nice to not only have a God who saves, but a God who knows and understands your pain? Do you want purpose and meaning to your life? Purpose to your pain and suffering? A purpose that is greater than yourself? Jesus is your only answer.

I pray that today God will lift the veil from your eyes and enlighten your heart to the truth of His Salvation that comes only through His Son so you can repent of your sin and be saved. "Salvation is found in no one else, for there is no other name under heaven given to mankind by which we must be saved" (Acts 4:12). And "I tell you, now is the time of God's favor, now is the day of salvation" (2 Corinthians 6:2).

Reference Notes

Introduction

1 Charles Martin, What If It's True: A Storyteller's Journey with Jesus, W Publishing, an imprint of Thomas Nelson, 2019

Chapter 1

1 Charles Spurgeon, *Morning and Evening;* Devotional material for the Morning of March 8th

2 Jen Wilkin, *Women of the Word* (Wheaten, Illinois: Crossway 2014) p. 27

3 John MacArthur, Jr., *The Power of Suffering* (Wheaton, Illinois: Victor Books, 1995) p. 23

4 A. W. Pink, *The Sovereignty of God,* rev. ed. (Edinburgh: Banner of Truth, 1961) pp. 20-23

5 Jerry Bridges, *Trusting God* (Colorado Springs, CO: NavPress, 1988) p. 69

6 J. I. Packer, "Providence", *The New Bible Dictionary* (London: InterVarsity, 1962), pp. 1050-1051

7 Jerry Bridges, *Trusting God* (Colorado Springs, CO: NavPress, 1988) p. 35

8 Robert A. Morey, *Fearing God* (Yorba Linda, CA: Davidson Press, 1999) p.20

9 James Robert White, *The Forgotten Trinity: Recovering the Heart of Christian Belief* (Bloomington, Minnesota: Bethany House Publishers, 1998) https://www.goodreads.com/author/quotes/9234007.James_R_White Accessed prior to 3/15/2022

10 Robert A. Morey, *Fearing God* (Yorba Linda, CA: Davidson Press, 1999) p. 40

Chapter 2

1   Josef Tson, The School of Suffering, http://articles.ochristian.com/article2624.shtml Accessed prior to 3/15/2022

2   https://biblehub.com/greek/5048.htm Accessed prior to 3/15/2022

3   Charles Spurgeon, Morning and Evening; Devotional material for the Morning of March 29

Chapter 3

1   Charles Spurgeon, *Morning and Evening*; Devotional material for the Morning of May 22nd

2   Gregg Allison, *50 Core Truths of the Christian Faith* (Grand Rapids, MI: Baker Books, 2018) p.267

3   Mary Wiley, *Everyday Theology*, (Nashville, TN: LifeWay Press, reprint 2020), p. 157

4   Charles Spurgeon, *Morning and Evening*, Devotional material for Evening of September 3rd

5   Charles Spurgeon, *Morning and Evening*, Devotional material for Evening of September 3rd

6   John Piper, *Future Grace*, (Colorado Springs, CO: Multnomah Books, 1995, 2012) p. 94-95

7   Hymn: 'Tis my Happiness Below, Words: William Cowper, Olney Hymns (London: W. Oliver, 1779), Music: Madrid (Carr) traditional Spanish tune. Arranged by Benjamin Carr, 1824, http://www.hymntime.com/tch/htm/t/i/m/y/timyhabe.htm Accessed prior to 3/15/2022

Chapter 4

1   Bryan Chapell, *Holiness By Grace* (Wheaton Illinois: Crossway Books, 2001) p. 160.

2   Samuel Bolton, The True Bonds of Christian Freedom https://gracequotes.org/author-quote/samuel-bolton/ Accessed prior to 3/15/2022

3   Charles Spurgeon, https://gracequotes.org/quote/it-is-never-said-whom-the-lord-loveth-he-enricheth-but-it-is-said-whom-the-lord-loveth-he-chasteneth/ Accessed prior to 3/15/2022

4   Hymn: Come Thou Fount, Words: Robert Robinson, 1758, Tune: "Nettleton", by John Wyeth, https://en.wikipedia.org/wiki/Come Thou Fount of Every Blessing Accessed prior to 3/15/2022

Chapter 5

1   John Piper, *Tsunami, Sovereignty, and Mercy*, Article found: https://www.desiringgod.org/articles/tsunami-sovereignty-and-mercy, Accessed prior to 3/15/2022
2   Joni Eareckson Tada, *Glorious Intruder: God's Presence in Life's Chaos*, (New York, NY: WaterBrook Multnomah, 1989) p. 48
3   *Greater Good Magazine: Science based insights for a meaningful life*, "How Comforting Others Helps You with Your Own Struggles" By Kira M. Newman, June 5, 2017 https://greatergood.berkeley.edu/article/item/how_comforting_others_helps_you_with_your_own_struggles Accessed prior to 3/15/2022
4   John Piper, Desiring God (Colorado Springs, CO: Multnomah Books, 2011) p. 341
5   Jerry Bridges, *Trusting God* (Colorado Springs, CO: NavPress, 1988) p. 113
6   John Piper, Desiring God daily devotion, April 4th, https://www.desiringgod.org/articles/god-strengthens-us-through-others Accessed prior to 3/15/2022

Chapter 6

1   Tony Reinke, Suffering Opens the Door for the Gospel, DesiringGod.org Accessed prior to 3/15/2022
2   Richard Wurmbrand, *Tortured for Christ*, https://www.goodreads.com/work/quotes/75922-tortured-for-christ Accessed prior to 3/15/2022
3   Tony Reinke, Suffering Opens the Door for the Gospel, DesiringGod.org Accessed prior to 3/15/2022
4   John Piper, *Desiring God* (Colorado Springs, CO: Multnomah Books, 2011) p. 269-270
5   Baptist Press, News Article, Romanian Josef Tson recounts God's grace amid suffering,https://www.baptistpress.com/resource-library/news/romanian-josef-tson-recounts-gods-grace-amid-suffering/ Accessed prior to 3/15/2022

6   James R. White, *Scripture Alone: Exploring the Bible's Accuracy, Authority, and Authenticity,* (Bloomington, MI: Bethany House Publishers 2004) https://www.goodreads.com/work/quotes/309183-scripture-alone-exploring-the-bibles-accuracy-authority-and-authentici, Accessed prior to 3/15/2022

7   Christianity Today, The 50 Countries Where It's Most Dangerous to Follow Jesus in 2021,https://www.opendoorsusa.org/christian-persecution/stories/13-christians-killed-every-day/ Accessed prior to 3/15/2022

Chapter 7

1   Jerry Bridges, *Trusting God* (Colorado Springs, CO: NavPress, 1988) p. 124
2   John Piper, *Finally Alive: What Happens when We are Born Again?* (United Kingdom: Christian Focus Publications, 2009)
3   John Piper, February 2, 2015 What Is Sin? The Essence and Root of All Sinning, Plenary Session – 2015 Conference for Pastors, Where Sin Increased: The Rebellion of Man and the Abundance of Grace, https://www.desiringgod.org/messages/what-is-sin-the-essence-and-root-of-all-sinning Accessed prior to 3/15/2022
4   Chris Tiegreen, *Why a Suffering World Makes Sense* (Grand Rapids, MI: Baker Publishing Group, 2006) p. 106
5   Andrew Murray, *Humility and Absolute Surrender* (Hendrickson Publishers, 2005) p.55

Chapter 8

1   Watchman Nee, *Journeying Towards the Spiritual: A Digest of the Spiritual Man in 42 Lessons* (New York, NY: Christian Fellowship Publishers, 2009) p.79
2   Charles Spurgeon, A Sermon (No. 1799), Delivered on Lord's-Day Morning, September 14th, 1884 https://archive.spurgeon.org/sermons/1799.php Accessed prior to 3/15/2022

Chapter 9

1   R.C. Sproul, *The Promises of God: Discovering the One Who Keeps His Word* (Colorado Springs, CO: David Cook, 2013) https://www.goodreads.

com/work/quotes/21542015-the-promises-of-god-discovering-the-one-who-keeps-his-word Accessed prior to 3/15/2022

2 Matthew Henry's Concise Commentary on Psalm 116:10-19, https://www.christianity.com/bible/commentary/mhc/psalm/116 Accessed prior to 3/15/2022

3 Charles Spurgeon, *Morning and Evening*, Devotional material for the Evening of November 19th

4 Timothy Keller, *Walking with God Through Pain and Suffering* (New York, NY: Riverhead Books, 2013) https://www.goodreads.com/work/quotes/24678714-walking-with-god-through-pain-and-suffering Accessed prior to 3/15/2022

5 Lindsey Tollefson, *Psalms for trials: Meditations of Praying the Psalms* (Moscow, Idaho: Cannon Press, 2018)

6 John Piper, Desiring God Daily Devotion, May 21, God Works for You, https://www.desiringgod.org/articles/god-works-for-you Accessed prior to 3/15/2022

7 Beauty for Ashes, Lyrics by Crystal Lewis, Album: Beauty for Ashes, Released 1996

8 Charles Spurgeon, Morning and Evening, Devotional material for the Morning of May 23rd

9 R.C. Sproul, *The R.C. Sproul Collection Volume 1: The Holiness of God / Chosen by God* (Tyndale House Publishers, Inc., 2017) p.364

Chapter 10

1 Charles Spurgeon, *Morning and Evening*, Devotional material for the Evening of August 17th

2 It Is Well With My Soul, lyrics by Horatio Spafford, composed by Philip Bliss (1876)

Epilogue

1 https://www.law.cornell.edu/wex/impute Accessed prior to 3/15/2022

2 John Piper, *Desiring God* (Colorado Springs, CO: Multnomah Books, 2011) p. 62-63